Helpful Household Hints

by
June King

Published by:
SANTA MONICA PRESS LLC
P.O. Box 1076
Santa Monica, CA 90406-1076
www.santamonicapress.com
1-800-784-9553

Printed in the United States

This book gives the reader a guide to the basics of maintaining a home. You should always follow the manufacturer's instructions to any tool or cleaning product, take appropriate safety precautions, and use your best judgment before undertaking any projects outlined in this book. Always make sure that your work area is safe and your tools and supplies are in proper working condition. All cleaning, repair and maintenance projects involve risk, and the publisher and the author take no responsibility for any injury or loss arising from the procedures or materials described in this book.

Publisher's Cataloging-in-Publication Data

King, June, 1955-
Helpful Household Hints
June King
224 pp
ISBN 0-9639946-3-8
Library of Congress Catalog Card Number 95-72710

1. Home Economics   2. House Cleaning.
3. Dwellings—Maintenance and Repair.
640.43

10 9 8 7 6 5 4 3 2

Contents

Introduction

How many times have you walked through your house, wishing that things could be more organized? How many times have you thought about the amount of time you could save doing chores if they would just go more smoothly? How many times have you wondered how much money you could save by maintaining things yourself, *before* professional repairmen needed to be called?

If you've thought about these things, then you're not alone. In fact, people all over the country are finally realizing that they can significantly increase their free time and their savings by putting a little extra effort into organizing their homes.

Within these pages, you will find hundreds of simple and timesaving tricks. Don't try to learn every trick in this book at once. Taking in too much at once will give you a kind of overload, and this is bound to make you not want to use any of the suggestions in the book. If you try two or three new things every week, then within a month you are bound to find that your chores take considerably less time to complete each day. This is the very reason why I wrote this book: the less time you have to spend cleaning your home, the more time you can spend enjoying it! Your home is your castle, so you shouldn't be a slave to it.

Unlike many other books on cleaning, which actively promote brand name products, I have shied away from that approach. I have discovered through a little ingenuity and experimentation that you can actually concoct some pretty potent cleansers with items that you have in your home right now! Whenever I do specify that a store bought cleanser needs to be used,

I have called it by its generic name (such as disinfectant), as you might already have a favorite brand that works best for you.

Cleaning your home does require some kind of an inventory of cleaning supplies, so I suggest you read through some of the entries in this book prior to doing your housework in order to get a good idea of what you will need. Whenever possible, I suggest using a homemade alternative to a store bought product, such as using an old toothbrush instead of an expensive scrub brush, but you will probably still find the need to go out and buy a few things. To help get you started, the following is a partial list of what you will need, without any kind of explanation (the explanations will be supplied in the appropriate entries):

- Rags (or old shirts or towels)
- Soft cloths (don't skimp on these; if I suggested using a soft cloth, then don't substitute something like an old shirt, which could be quite abrasive)
- Sponges
- A broom
- A mop
- Rubber gloves
- A ladder
- A bucket
- Dishwashing detergent
- Disinfectant
- Bleach
- Laundry detergent
- Cleansers (you should have a variety on hand, each of which can be used to clean different household items)
- A toothbrush

- Toothpaste
- Yogurt
- Dry spotter
- Salt
- Worcestershire sauce
- Steel wool
- Vinegar
- An iron

I realize that you are probably scratching your head about some of the "cleaning supplies" on this list, such as yogurt and Worcestershire sauce, but they are not jokes, and you will soon discover how useful they can be; many people mistakenly believe that only special (and expensive) cleansers will do the trick with certain stains, but this couldn't be further from the truth!

Most importantly, while I have never had any problems with the cleaning methods I outline in these pages, it is vital that you always test any new cleaning material before using it. This is especially true when trying out a stain remover for the first time. Use the ingredients I suggest on a small piece of the article in question before going to town. If it's a shirt you're cleaning, try the concoction on the bottom corner of the shirt to make sure it doesn't damage the fabric. If you're cleaning a floor, countertop, piece of furniture, etc., be sure to test the cleaning material on a small portion of the item before you begin spreading it all over.

In addition to proper cleaning supplies, it is absolutely necessary that every home have at least a basic tool kit. You simply cannot maintain your home properly without tools. And if you've just moved in, you will find that some repairs and/or upgrades will be necessary right away, and these will require some work.

Sure, you could always hire a handyman or carpenter to tend to it, but that's not always affordable. Moreover, as you will see in the chapter on Household Repair and Maintenance, much of this work is simple, and can be performed with just a little instruction and the basic tools. Plus, it's more satisfying when you do it yourself. In any case, you should have access to the following tools. Instead of buying all of them, think about splitting the cost with a neighbor or two. The basics:

• A claw hammer. This is your standard hammer, with a pair of claws on the back of the head. You can find small ones for around five dollars, but it's a good investment to spend $15 to $20 on a good, sturdy one that won't bend your nails. Look for a one-pound head and a handle made of either steel or fiberglass. This will serve you in both minor and major jobs, and should last many, many years.

• A tape measure. This is, of course, for measuring distances in your house: of floors, walls, door height, spacing between nails for hanging shelves and pictures, and myriad other uses. Make sure you buy one that clips onto your belt, with tape that is at least 3/4 inches wide and 15 feet long. This should cost you about $12.

• Screwdrivers. These are probably the most used—and thus, abused—tools in your household, so make sure you buy the sturdiest models you can afford, preferably with hardened steel tips and a long shank for better torque. A set of four should suffice for most household jobs—two with slotted heads and two with Phillips heads, in small and medium sizes. The set should run you about $12.

9

• Locking pliers. The all-purpose household tool, it serves as a clamp, a wrench (for which it is often confused), a wire cutter, and even, on occasion, as a sturdy set of pliers. A must for both a tool kit and, perhaps, the kitchen drawer. Cost: about $12.

• Needle-nose pliers. This tool often comes with wire cutters built into the jaws, so it's a two-for-one deal already. Its purpose is primarily for clamping in tight, hard-to-reach spaces. An eight-inch size is about right. Good ones cost about $10.

• Slip-jaw pliers. These look very much like locking pliers, but the difference is that you can adjust the width of the mouth, depending on the size of the job. It's a good idea to get a small (about six-and-a-half inches) and a medium (ten inches) size. The small one handles most household jobs, while the larger one can tackle more serious tasks, such as plumbing repairs. These can also substitute for a good wrench in a pinch. The good ones will cost about $10 (small) and $12 (medium).

• Adjustable wrenches. Buy two of these: a six-inch and a ten-inch, just like with the slip-jaw pliers; and also just like those, the small one will handle the small repairs, the larger one for loosening the more heavy-duty bolts and automotive jobs. Here again, buy a name-brand you can trust, and they will last you a long, long time.

• Extension Cords. If you're going to fix something, fix it right. Likewise, to protect your job, you'll often need a good extension cord to carry the current. The longer the cord, the heavier its gauge should be; otherwise, a drop in voltage could occur and short out your appliance. A grounded thirty-foot cord with sixteen-gauge wire will suit most projects, and only cost about $15.

• Trouble light. This is a bulb in a cage that can be attached at the end of the extension cord, for working in the dark. Cost: about $12.

• Flashlights. Every home should have several— one for every room. In natural disasters, such as earth-quakes, heavy storms, hurricanes and the like, it's very common to lose all power in the house, necessitating the use of a flashlight. (Never light candles if your house has a gas line—fire and fumes equals tragedy!) Spend a little more on sturdy flashlights—with steel frames and black rubber handles (a set of four will cost about $20). And make sure the batteries are kept fresh.

• Paintbrushes. They come in all sizes, shapes and fibers, so you might want to consider a set, depend-ing on your needs. For painting walls or other large areas, choose a straight cut; for touch-up work, a ta-pered cut. For latex paint, polyester bristles are best; for oil paint, hog bristle brushes. If you buy only one, however, make it a polyester with a straight cut, as it's more versatile. In any case, do not ever skimp on price—in the world of paintbrushes, quality counts a great deal, as a cheap model will cost you more dearly in frustration, with bristles falling out at inopportune times, the cut not holding its shape, etc. Spend a little more and your job will be easy.

• Handsaw. For most work around the house and yard, a ten-point saw will do just fine (this means it has ten teeth per inch): it will cut quickly enough for a rough cut and finely enough for most jobs to look fin-ished. Cost: about $18.

• Hacksaw. This tool is extremely useful, especially for its price. You can use it to cut through pipes, ce-ramic tile, or any number of hard objects. When shop-ping, buy the most rigid one you can find—if it bends

11

the least bit, it's no good. Also make sure it's adjustable for both straight cuts or cuts at a 45-degree angle, and can accept either ten-inch or twelve-inch blades. At just under $20, it's a heck of a deal.

• Chisels. These tools are for chipping out blocks of material—be it wood, drywall or even concrete or metal—particularly in hard-to-reach places. The most useful blade sizes for household purposes are 1/4-inch and 3/4-inch; for the harder substances, a cold chisel is necessary. You should also invest in a sharpening stone, since chisels are easily blunted. A five-by-two-inch stone should suffice, but make sure it's two sided—one side coarse, one fine (this can also be used to sharpen knives). The whole set should cost about $35.

• Knives. Two important knives should be in every tool kit: a putty knife and a retractable utility blade knife. The former is large and flat, perfect for applying spackle, scraping paint, stripping furniture polish, or patting down wallpaper. The latter is for any old need: cutting wallpaper, opening containers, and who knows what else. Cost for both together: about $15.

Another important thing you need to keep in mind when cleaning and maintaining your home is safety. Here are a few tips:

1. Be careful whenever dealing with electricity. Don't get water near electrical outlets, lamps, or any other electrical products. There is enough power in a regular wall socket to *kill* someone!

2. Ladders can be very dangerous. Never work on a ladder without someone else being present. If you fall,

someone should be nearby to assist you. Regardless, most ladders require a second person to hold them steady. There are several types of cleaning which will almost definitely require you to use ladders, such as washing your ceiling or your outside walls, so keep this safety tip in mind. Incidentally, if someone does fall from a ladder and seems to be having difficulty moving, then don't move them or you could cause even more serious damage! Call for help from the appropriate authorities.

3. Be wary of toxic fumes. Most cleaning products are chemicals. Most chemicals are harmful to humans when found in large doses. Some products are only mildly toxic, such as most disinfectants, whereas others are highly toxic, such as oven cleaners. Always read labels for any warnings, and always work in well ventilated work areas.

4. When lifting heavy objects, such as furniture, always lift with the knees, not with the back. In other words, lower yourself into a crouching position and raise the object as you straighten your legs. If you simply bend over to pick up an object, then you could throw your back out very badly when standing upright again.

5. Some chemicals are flammable. Read the labels carefully regarding the proper storage and handling of such chemicals. We've all heard funny stories about things spontaneously combusting, but with cleansers this is no joke! In fact, I highly recommend you invest in a fire extinguisher if you don't already have one.

6. Learn how to turn off the electricity in your home at the circuit breaker. If you ever drop any electrical item into a bucket of water, then the only safe way to remove it is by shutting off its flow of electricity. Knowing which circuits are controlled by which breakers is an important thing to know anyway, in case one of your fuses ever blows.

7. Learn how to treat physical contact with the cleansers you use. If some disinfectant ever got in your eye, would you know what to do? How about if some spilled on your skin? The warning labels have very precise directions on what should be done, so do yourself a favor and read them. I also suggest you invest in a pair of rubber gloves, so that you can keep your hands clean and free of any chemicals.

After reading this book, you'll be delighted to know all the different ways that you can make your chores and daily activities go by more quickly. You will learn, for example, how to rearrange your bathroom in such a way that you and your loved ones can prepare yourselves for the day in a more timely fashion, allowing you to sleep in later or even spend some more quality time together around the breakfast table. You will also discover ingenious ways of reducing your spending, such as saving money on both food and energy bills by keeping your refrigerator and freezer fully stocked!

You might be asking yourself if you are capable of re-organizing your household so drastically as to achieve results like these. But rest assured, the kinds of changes you need to make are so minor that they are well within the reach of anyone. Many of the tasks can be turned into group efforts, bringing your whole family together for fun activities such as garage sales. Isn't it wonderful to know that by working together, your family members can create even more free time to spend with each other?

If you do find yourself needing help, then there are plenty of convenient channels you can go through in order to hire a responsible person. This book will show you how to find the right person for the job, helping you to insure that you can place confidence in your hired help.

Hopefully, once you have finished looking through these pages, you will understand how to turn your household into a better home. You will know how to save both time and money, which can be a reward for the entire family! Good luck!

Solving the Mystery of Time

The most important element that organizational plans have in common with one another is time. It does take a bit of time to work through the procedures which have been outlined in this book, and without a plan to maximize your time, you will never be able to accomplish all of the things you need to do in order to organize your household. Here is a solid plan of attack to solving the mystery of time:

1) Every night before you go to bed, take a few minutes to make a list of "things to do" during the following day. By keeping such a daily calendar at your bedside, and by religiously making entries night after night until it is an established routine, you will be well on the road to having an efficient, organized schedule that saves you time.

2) Rank the things you have to do in order of importance. For instance, if you are throwing a dinner party, everything associated with that party should take precedence over such tasks as picking up the dry cleaning and other jobs which can easily be put off for a day or two (unless you have nothing to wear to your party, of course!).

3) Now comes the most challenging part: how to arrange your daily tasks into a manageable order. Well, you've already taken a major step simply by ranking the jobs in order of significance. Once you have done this, follow these steps:

a) Figure out approximately how long it will take you to perform each task.

b) Consolidate the jobs into like groups —for instance, if you have to go to the bank and the market, and these two places are right around the corner from each other, then make sure you group them together instead of separating them by the trip across town you must make to meet with the doctor.

c) Be practical with your time-slotting. If you need to perform a task such as weeding the garden and it is the middle of summer, do the task in the early morning or evening hours when the temperature is not so hot; as for equipment-related tasks, such as sanding your wood floors, if the sander is only available at a certain time of day, make sure that you slot this job in at the time when the sander is available. Remember, a little common sense goes a long way when planning out your day!

d) Make efficient use of small chunks of time. Create a list of jobs that take only a few minutes to perform, such as making an appointment over the phone. When you find yourself with a few extra minute on your hands, simply consult your "things to do" list and perform one of these minor tasks.

Timesaving Hints

Take advantage of pick-up and delivery services whenever possible. Additionally, a home service handyman can perform many small tasks for a minimal fee that will save you bundles of time!

Prepare certain functions such as making breakfast, dressing for the following day and gathering together the materials for a report you have to make, the night before you have to do them. By laying out the items you need for the following day every evening, you will save yourself valuable time in he morning—time you can put to other uses!

Take advantage of modern technology! There are many inventions, appliances, and other time saving devices that are meant for people trying to save time and become better organized. Easy-care fabrics, electric appliances and the like should be utilized whenever possible.

Try to perform two tasks at one time. For instance, you might be able to cook or do laundry while talking on the telephone or making an appointment.

Place twenty, one hour jobs (such as filing or ironing) on individual slips of paper and place them into a bowl. Then place five pleasurable one hour activities (such as reading or sunbathing) on individual pieces of paper and mix them into the bowl with the other jobs. Every day pick a piece of paper out of the bowl and perform that task, be it work or play!

Arrange car pools, shopping errands and baby sitting chores with family, friends, and neighbors in order to save time. As most top corporations know, pooling together resources is always the most efficient use of time.

Home cleaning services or a maid is another way to save valuable time while keeping a clean, neat and organized household. Consider sharing a maid with a neighbor in order to minimize the cost.

Plan visits to the bank, market and other places where there are often long lines, during off-peak hours when lines are shorter.

The Kitchen

The kitchen is one of the most important rooms in any household, but unfortunately most people just don't keep it clean and organized. They have to waste precious time every morning while preparing breakfast (we all know *exactly* how it feels to stare at our watches while we scramble through the refrigerator looking for something to eat, just wishing that we had five extra minutes before departing for work). And there is nothing worse than interrupting quality family time because you haven't planned your dinner in advance, and it takes you over an hour to prepare it. Plus, how many hours have you wasted while trying to keep your kitchen clean?

But don't fret! The simple tips you will find within this chapter are sure to make your kitchen a cleaner, better organized, and a more pleasurable room in which to spend your time.

An Organizational Plan of Attack

1) Empty out all of your cupboards, closets, drawers, window sills, and any place else where kitchen items have found a home (i.e. the top of your refrigerator).

2) Place these items into common groupings, such as silverware, dishes, glasses, pots and pans, snacks, spices, canned goods, etc.

3) Discard all broken and/or chipped items as well as things which you haven't used for ages and will realistically never use again. These items should be given to a charitable organization. You might try placing materials that are only used on special occasions (i.e.

20

canning equipment, holiday cooking utensils, etc.) into storage areas in other parts of your home.

4) Wipe down all shelves, counters and drawers, and place new shelf paper on areas which are in need of such a touch.

5) Create specially designated areas for each of your groupings and place them in various spots around you kitchen according to the following definitions:

a) Tableware: includes everything that would possibly go onto your dining or kitchen table—dishes, glasses, silverware, serving bowls and dishes, salt and pepper shakers, containers, table decorations, etc. Place these items as close to the dining or kitchen table as possible.

b) Cooking: includes everything you will use while preparing food—herbs, oils, dry sauces, flour, sweeteners, baking soda and powder, nuts, spices, food coloring, shortening, etc. Place these items adjacent to the countertop where you prepare your meals.

c) Utensils: includes everything you will use while cooking or when preparing to cook—tongs, spatulas, large spoons and forks, whisks, butcher's knives, etc. Place these items near the stove or the countertop where you prepare food.

d) Pots and Pans: all of your pots, pans, small appliances, baking sheets, griddles, etc., should be placed near your oven.

e) Pantry: obviously, this is the spot for all of your canned and dry foods, along with some backup supplies that did not fit into the cooking area. Try to divide these items up into breakfast, lunch, dinner, and snack foods.

f) Refrigerator: try to keep the items you use most often as close to the front of the refrigerator's racks as possible. Like the other areas of your kitchen, group foods together according to similarity and usage. Cheeses, sodas, jams, condiments and the like are just a few of the most common groupings.

g) Cleanup: includes everything you would not only use to clean up the kitchen, but the entire household as well—soap, sponges, bucket, rags, detergent, cleaning formulas, etc. The best place for these items is either under the sink or in a spare cupboard.

h) Miscellaneous: items such as storage bags, lunch sacks, aluminum foil, etc. should be placed in a spare drawer.

6) Look around your kitchen before you actually start putting things on the shelves. Give yourself a little time, walk around and "practice" making your favorite dishes. The cooking utensils and ingredients you use most often should be located in places that are easy to get to. Be creative!

7) When placing items on the shelves, put heavier things, such as pots and pans, closer to the ground, and lighter things, such as napkins, up high. Although bottles are usually quite light, they should still be placed closer to the ground, in order to reduce the risk of shattering.

8) After you have put away all of your kitchen belongings into the areas that have been designated above, you may find items particular to your way of life that still haven't found a home. This is where your own ingenuity comes into play. Using the same logic which I have displayed above, create your own categories and groupings and find a neat space for these personal items that will allow easy access.

Cleaning

Sparkling Racks

If you've ever used one of those canned oven cleaners, then you are aware that they are not suited for cleaning your oven racks. So how exactly are you supposed to clean your oven racks? I find the best way is simply to put them in your bathtub or a large bucket, cover them with scalding hot water, and add a small dose of ammonia. Be careful, as the ammonia will create some powerful fumes. Leave the racks in the water for at least four hours, and then scrub all the residue off with steel wool. Once you have done this, don't forget to rinse the rack thoroughly, as ammonia is certainly toxic, and you don't want any getting on your food.

Fabulous Faucets

Faucets and other fixtures can be some of the most beautiful elements of any kitchen, but when they start to get dirty, then their luster no longer illuminates the room. The best way to deal with this problem is to mix vinegar and baking soda together in a bowl and apply the mixture liberally to the fixture. Let it work its way into the layer of dirt for an hour of two, and then get ready to scrub hard.

Precious Pots

If you like to cook, then you understand the joy that can come from owning a set of fabulous and shiny pots, made out of a material such as aluminum or brass. The only problem with these great cookware sets is that their color begins to fade after only a few uses, and they no longer sparkle when you hang them on your wall with pride. There are, however, a few tricks you can use to rejuvenate them. If your pots are brass, then drench them in Worcestershire sauce and scrub away with a piece of steel wool (this trick also works splendidly for brass doorknobs). If they are made of aluminum, then pour some vinegar inside them and put them on your stove burners. Turn up the heat, so the vinegar boils for a few minutes, and then turn off the heat, but leave the pans on the warm burners for one or two hours. If you wash the pan again, then much of its original luster will return.

Clean Counters

Some kitchens feature counter-tops made of Formica. Formica comes either in a matte finish or a shiny finish. No matter which type you have in your home, it is a cinch to clean! Simply use an old shirt or a sponge that has been soaked in warm water. To handle any particularly pesky areas, you might want to try using either club soda or lemon juice. Never use any kind of soap, as chemicals can easily destroy the surface of Formica.

Stainless Steel Sinks

If you are very lucky, then your kitchen comes equipped with an industrial quality stainless steel sink (I am very envious of you). These sinks truly live up to their name, except that water spots are very glaring on their surface. I find that vinegar is the best way to rid your sink of these ugly spots, but you must then also apply a coating of club soda, as this will make it glisten like new. Always dry the fixture thoroughly after this, or all your hard work will have been wasted; the club soda will form new spots if allowed to air dry in the sink.

Clean Pipes

We all know that annoying feeling of staring down into a kitchen sink that won't drain. In order to prevent your pipes from clogging up, there are a few simple precautions to take. First, never wash oil or fat down the drain; wait for it to solidify and throw it out instead. Second, brush any pieces of food (even the small crumbs!) into the garbage rather than letting them go down the drain. One of the best ways to get rid of a clog that is already in your drain is to pour a mixture of salt and boiling water into it.

Clean Frying

To keep oil from splashing out of your frying pan and onto your beautiful stove, use a metal strainer or colander as a lid. The oil will stay in, but the hot air will find its way out through the holes.

Good, Clean Trash

There's nothing quite as smelly as a dirty garbage disposal, but it's quite simple to make the problem go away. Toss in a few rinds from citrus fruits and turn the disposal on. An even more powerful method is to make a batch of ice cubes with a healthy dose of vinegar in them; pour the cubes down the drain and turn it on. The smell will disappear almost immediately! Before doing this, however, you should test the dis-

25

posal with one or two cubes, to make sure that it is strong enough.

Sticky Silverware

Here's a problem that many people encounter: they wash their silverware very carefully, but then it gets dirty and sticky in the drawer. The best way to handle this problem is by fixing the drawer. Contact paper is a very inexpensive and simple method of covering the insides of drawers and closet shelves. Contact paper is also extremely easy to clean, thereby eliminating the dirt that builds up so quickly on silverware.

Correct Contact

If you do decide to line your drawers and shelves with contact paper, then here's a little hint to make your chore easier: make the piece of paper slightly smaller than the drawer it is meant to cover. That way, when it comes time to replace the paper, you will have an exposed edge to grab onto in order to remove it! Don't ever simply place a new layer of contact paper over an old one, as you will be covering up a dirty (and potentially germ-infected) mess. This mess will eventually soak through the new layer.

Clean Cupboards

Before lining your shelves or drawers with contact paper, you should make sure that they are thoroughly cleaned, inside and out. Rubbing alcohol is a great cleanser for cutting down grease that might have accumulated on the bottom of drawers, and it is also perfect for getting rid of smudges and stains on the handles. Rubbing alcohol has a way of actually penetrating the stains and destroying them from within.

Practical Paper

Paper towels are one of the best ways of cleaning up simple spills in the kitchen. But paper towels can be expensive, so use some common sense before utilizing them. First, ask yourself if the spill could easily be removed with a sponge (without damaging the sponge, of course, which could be quite costly). If the spill isn't very sticky, but shouldn't be wiped with a sponge, use a cheaper brand of paper towel. If the spill is very sticky, then (and only then) break out the expensive paper towels, which are generally the most absorbent. Paper towels are only practical when used economically!

Goodbye Garbage!

Yuck! What's that horrible smell in the kitchen? It's coming from the sink. It must be the garbage disposal! How can I clean it so it won't smell? The answer to this question is far easier than most people realize. Simply fill your sink up with water and squeeze the juice of a lemon into it. Then turn on your disposal, and let all the water drain past it. The smell will be gone in a jiffy.

Cutting Germs

It is important to keep your cutting board clean, as germs can easily be transferred from one piece of food to another on the board. If you use a clever to cut your food, which forces you to hack at it when you cut, then you might make tiny gouges in the surface of your cutting board. These should be sanded down every now and then, in order to prevent food particles from becoming stuck within them. You should also wipe down your cutting board with vegetable oil fairly regularly, as this will help moisturize the wood and help prevent any gouges from occurring.

Clean Racks

Everyone knows how to clean their dishes, but few people realize that their dish rack can get dirty too. It truly defeats the point of washing your dishes if you dry them on something disgusting and dirty! Go to the kitchen and wash yours with soap and hot water right away! Then, every day before washing the dishes, rinse the rack with hot water to keep it sanitary.

The Little Things

With cleaning, as with life in general, it is attention to detail, to the little things, that really counts. So if you want your kitchen to look clean, then you have to pay attention to the small details. Make sure all the cupboards are kept shut when no one is removing something from them. Take dishes off of the dish rack as soon as they have dried, and never let a large amount of dirty dishes pile up in the sink. Hide power cords in such a way that they don't dangle in plain view. And keep the front of your refrigerator clean! It's wonderful to show your love and pride for your child by displaying their straight-A report card, but take it down after a month or so!

Radiant Reflectors

Those little metal disks that fit under your burners are called reflectors, because they reflect heat upward toward the pot. As you probably already know, these reflectors get dirty just about every time you use them, and if you wait a long time before cleaning them, then the stains harden and are extremely difficult to remove. As such, I suggest you wrap you reflectors in aluminum foil. When the foil starts to get too dirty (which will happen about every week or so), simply remove it and put on a new layer. If you don't like the way the aluminum foil looks on your oven, and would rather be able to see the reflectors themselves, then you will have to soak them in a pot of extremely hot water and dishwashing detergent as frequently as you would have had to remove the foil. You might have to also use a bit of elbow grease, even after they have soaked for a few hours, but they usually come clean.

Appliances
Fresh Refrigerators
Keeping your refrigerator smelling fresh can be one the biggest nuisances you will ever face in your kitchen. The best way to eliminate such foul smells is to place a few charcoal briquettes on a plate in the refrigerator. When the pieces of charcoal seem to stop working, simply warm them in a frying pan for a few minutes.

Cold is Cheap
Freezers work most efficiently, and therefore least expensively, when they are extremely full. Put as much food in it as you can in order to reduce your energy bill. This might also reduce your grocery bill, as buying in bulk is always cheaper and quicker (you don't have to make as many trips to the store).

Clean Refrigerators are Happy Refrigerators
Removing dust from beneath your refrigerator is one of the easiest ways to make it last for years and years. You should move it every three months so that you can give it a good cleaning (that pesky dirt really sticks to the bottom!), but don't forget to unplug it to reduce the risk of shock. Doing this will save you a great deal

of time and money, as your refrigerator will better regulate its temperature, allowing foods to stay fresh for longer—that means you won't have to go to the grocery store as often!

Dusty Coils

Check for dust on the back coils. Too much dirt and lint collected on the coils will force them to work harder to do their cooling job, and so use up more energy. It's a good idea to take an old paintbrush or hand vacuum cleaner and brush off any dust periodically.

Fridge Follies

If you've ever tried to clean under your refrigerator without moving it, then you know what a comedic performance this can turn into. I find that the best way to do this is to simply put some pantyhose over a broom handle and use this as a duster. But there is no avoiding it; sooner or later you will have to move the fridge and clean under there. As the intake fans of most refrigerators are located at the bottom of the unit, don't be surprised to find a lot of dust under there!

Soggy Defrosting

Defrosting a freezer can be such a bother if you have to wipe it out. A quicker and easier method is to line the bottom of your freezer with a few absorbent towels. The towels will soak up all the water when you defrost the freezer.

Dollar Bill

First, check the weather stripping, which is like the insulation that contains the cold air on the inside. Too much cold air escaping means a refrigerator that doesn't keep food cold enough. To compensate, you may be turning the control too high, which in turn consumes too much energy. To check the weather stripping, open the refrigerator door, place a dollar bill in it and shut the door. If it sticks, and it's reasonably difficult to pull out, your weather stripping is good. If it's too easy to pull out, or falls, the weather stripping should be replaced.

Condensation Tray

If you have a self-defrosting refrigerator, check the condensation tray at least four times a year. This tray is usually hidden at the bottom front of the refrigerator, perhaps concealed by the base trim. It collects moisture from the defrosting device, which liquifies. If neglected, the water will overflow and perhaps even grow mold from stillness, which can cause health problems and possibly infect your food.

Blender Blues

I find that the blender is one of the greatest modern conveniences that I have in my kitchen, and I can't imagine whipping up a great meal without using it. But those darned blades can be so hard to wash, not to mention the glass or plastic jug of the blender itself. I find that the best way to clean it is to fill it about two-thirds of the way up with water, add a little bit of dishwashing detergent, turn the blender on, and let it wash itself! Afterwards, all that you will need to do is rinse with cold water.

Microwave Management

Microwaves are such common fixtures in modern homes that we tend to forget what sophisticated pieces of machinery they really are! As such, you should always exercise great caution when cleaning them. Your owner's manual probably has several suggestions for keeping it clean. If not, then I suggest that you wipe down the interior with a damp cloth after each use. This will prevent any stains from setting in. Always remember to dry it off with another towel after you have cleaned it, removing any and all excess water.

Microwave Safe?

The microwave is one of the greatest conveniences available in modern kitchens, but sometimes it's hard to tell if your dishes are microwave safe. The best way to test a dish is to put it in the microwave with a measuring cup filled with water. Heat for one minute at the highest power. Check the temperature of each; if the dish is cold and the water hot, then the dish is microwave safe.

Golden Brown

The toast is burning! To avoid this early-morning nightmare, make sure that the crumb tray in the bottom of your toaster is kept clean. This will prevent your toast from getting burned, thus saving you quite a bit of time and money every morning.

Self-Cleaning Solutions

If you have a self-cleaning oven, then you are probably delighted that such a wonderful, timesaving device was ever invented. But if your oven is an older model, then it might be having trouble maintaining the high temperatures it needs to clean itself adequately. A simple way to solve this problem is to put a pan filled with water in the oven at 400-degrees for about half an hour. I honestly can't tell you why this works, but it often does. Carefully remove the pan (you don't want to spill a pan of scalding water all over you!), and then try the self-cleaning function again.

Clean Burning

Cooking with gas is one of the most economical ways to prepare your food. But burners can easily become clogged, thereby decreasing their efficiency and increasing your gas bill (a yellow flame, as opposed to blue, is a sure sign of a clog). To clean them, use a toothbrush to remove any dirt that is stopping up any of the holes. But never do this with the gas turned on!

Smooth Blending

If you have one of those European style blenders (you know, the one with the two whisks that beat into a bowl), then you probably never use it because of the horrible mess it can make. To prevent the whisks from spraying your whole kitchen with batter or any other mixture you are blending, simply apply a small amount of nonstick spray to them. This will ensure that the batter keeps "falling" back into the bowl.

I Didn't Do It!

We all know the feeling. The coffee maker just won't work, no matter what you do. The only thing that anyone will say is, "I didn't do it!" Well before you call the repairman, here are a few things you can check for yourself. Is the fuse blown? Is the outlet at fault (check this by plugging in something that you know works)? Is the appliance plugged into the socket and turned on? Is the plug coming loose from the wire (this one is very important for all you naughty people who unplug things by pulling on the cord, rather than on the plug—don't try to fix this yourself)?

Food and Utensil Storage

Old Enough to Date

It can become very confusing to try and figure out which of your leftovers are oldest and should be eaten first. This problem can be remedied by a small pieces of paper with the date that you originally cooked the dish written on it. Simply tape the piece of paper to the container in which you're storing the leftover, and *voila*!

Where Did I Put That?

It seems like you can waste hours hunting and poking through a disorganized refrigerator, looking for different food items. To save yourself some time in the future, take one afternoon to completely reorganize your refrigerator. Group all of the similar items in one area. Put the taller ones *behind* the shorter ones, so that you will have no trouble seeing both (I hate it when I can't see what's behind that mayonnaise jar!). Until you have memorized your new plan, you might even want to make a little map or chart for yourself. This might sound silly at first, but in the long run you'll love it.

Fresh and Crispy

Let's face it, vegetables are always best when they are freshest, but there are certain things you can do to increase their storage life. Before you freeze them, most vegetables need to be blanched, and potatoes need to be cooked entirely. Greens will lose most of their crispness once frozen, so they must be cooked before eating.

No More Scratches

It's usually most convenient to stack your dishes and frying pans, as this can save a lot of space. But if you're not careful when reaching for a pan or plate, you can easily scratch the one beneath it. That's why you should try separating each with a disposable foam plate. You might try using paper plates, or even extra strong paper towels, but neither of these will last as long as foam.

Uncanny Idea

You should keep canned foods away from extreme temperatures; don't store them next to the oven, for example. Don't ever open a can of food that has any rust on it—just throw it out, because it might be tainted. Also, when opening a can, if you hear a strong hissing noise, like the sound of steam escaping, then throw it out, because it has definitely gone bad. If you're eating a can of food that has a considerable amount of fat in it, but you want to reduce the fat you intake, then here's a neat idea. Open the can and put it in the refrigerator for about an hour or two. The fat will all solidify, and you can lift it out with a spoon.

Ordered Utensils

Making sense out of your utensil drawers can be a nightmare! Well, here are three tips to make it a little easier for you. First, try buying a rotating tie rack that you can put on the counter, from which you can hang utensils that have holes in their handles, such as ladles and certain knives. Next, put all of your table flatware in a cup or jar on the counter, so that they are within easy reach at mealtime. Finally, to stop any utensils that are in drawers from rattling, try lining the drawer with Styrofoam.

Fish Facts

If you buy fresh fish that has not been frozen, then never freeze it (that would defeat the whole purpose of buying it fresh). It can be stored for about half a day in the refrigerator. Fill a colander with ice, and put the fish in the ice. Always keep a bowl underneath to catch ice water as it melts and drips through the holes.

Spicy Ideas

Sometimes it seems like it takes hours to search through a spice rack to find the spices you need. A simple idea to make things quicker for you is to place them on the rack alphabetically. If you think that you're not going to use a spice very often, then put it in the refrigerator to keep it fresh.

Screwy Ideas

Foods that come in cardboard boxes or non-resealable bags are easy prey for household pests, bacteria, and even curious pets. As such, it's a good idea to buy a large supply of storage containers with screw-on lids.

Safe China

Most people use their china very rarely. If you have kept your china in a closet or cupboard for a long time, then let it sit out for an hour before using it. This will prevent it from being damaged by extremely hot or cold food or drink. In fact, you might not want to store your china away at all, as it is thought that china actually gets stronger the more you use it.

Fresh Desserts

Desserts such as pies can be easily frozen and reheated later. The secret is to keep it looking as fresh and beautiful as when it first came out of the oven. To do this, take an empty pie pan and cover your pie with it. Tape the empty pan in place, and your delicious dessert will not get squashed, even if it gets bumped while in the freezer.

Fresh-Brewed Taste
Gourmet coffee can be very expensive. You can reduce the price by buying it in bulk. To keep it tasting just as fresh as the day you bought it, store the excess coffee in an airtight container in the freezer.

Tightly Sealed
Even if you store foods in specially made storage containers in your refrigerator, you still might find that foods don't last as long as you want them to. This is probably due to lids that are not perfectly airtight. An easy remedy is to cover the top of the container with plastic wrap before screwing the lid in place. This will also keep your refrigerator smelling fresher.

Wonderful Wine
If you like to drink wine every now and then, here are a few tips for storing your wine. Always lay the bottle flat on its side, rather than keeping it upright. This way the wine will coat the bottom of the cork, preventing air from getting in and spoiling it. Once you have drunk the wine, keep the corks and the bottles, as they make excellent storage containers. Not only are they great for liquids, such as oil and vinegar, but you can also fill them with snacks like unpopped popcorn or candy.

Fresher Bread
Don't you hate opening up a bag of bread and finding mold inside? To enjoy your bread longer, leave no more than half a loaf out. The rest should be kept in

the freezer. This is especially useful if you buy bread in bulk, which always saves you plenty of money. Once the bread defrosts, it can either be toasted or eaten as is.

Get into Habits

Let's face it, bad habits are hard to break, and good habits are even harder to form. How many of us really follow the old rule "Clean as you cook?" Here's a way to keep your kitchen organized, even under heavy use. Once you have found the perfect storage areas, using the various methods outlined above, make a chart for yourself to help you memorize everything's location. While you are cooking, simply put each item, such as a spice jar, in a box next to the stove once you are done with it. This will keep your counter space open, and when you're done, you can quickly return everything from the box to its rightful place.

Cooking

Sweet Smelling Onions

Onions make your food smell delicious, but they make your hands smell awful. The best way to rid your fingers of their scent is first to dab them in a bowl of vinegar. Vinegar far overpowers the smell of onions, and it is much easier to wash out when you are done. The vinegar from your fingers even adds an interesting sharpness to the taste of the onions.

Fruit Juice Cubes

On a hot summer day, there's nothing like a glass of fruit juice on the rocks. But as the ice begins to melt, it makes your beverage watery. To avoid this problem, simply make ice cubes from your favorite fruit juices.

That way, when the ice melts, it will simply increase the amount of beverage in your glass.

Juicy Lemons

Squeezing lemon into your favorite beverage or food is a wonderful way to increase its natural flavors. But lemons can be expensive, and they never seem to have very much juice in them. To get double the amount of juice from your lemon (or any other citrus fruit, for that matter), simply heat it up! Either put it in the microwave for a minute or so, or place it in a pot of hot water. Careful not to burn your hands!

Down the Drain

How many times have you put a bowl on the counter, dropped your ingredients into the bowl, and started mixing it with a spoon, only to find your mixture spilling everywhere? To prevent this sloppy situation, and the time that you have to spend cleaning it up, place the bowl in the sink. That way, there's no mess caused by any spills.

Easy Greasy

Always keep the paper wrapping that comes with a pat of butter or margarine. Whenever a recipe calls for you to grease a pan, simply wipe the wrapper over the pan!

Good Grating

Freshly grated cheeses and vegetables are so much more appetizing and appealing than pre-grated foods. But sometimes it can be difficult to grate food yourself. To make this task easier, grate vegetables and cheeses as soon as you remove them from the refrigerator, so they will be a little firmer. When you're done grating, brush any particles of food out of the holes with a basting brush; that way, there's no waste.

Tender Victuals

Many recipes with beef or pork call for you to tenderize the meat. There are two great ways for you to do this. First, take the back of a clever (or any other heavy utensil) and hammer it against the meat. Or second, if the meat is cut thin, marinate it in a bowl filled with either lemon juice or wine vinegar. Tenderizing by marinating also brings out and enhances the flavor of your dishes.

Smells Fishy

Let's face it, as delicious as sea food may be, raw fish makes your hands smell bad! To prevent the smell from sticking to your fingers while you prepare your seafood, keep the fish in ice water. Extremely cold fish will still smell a little, but far less than if the fish gets warm.

Turkey Dinner

Everyone seems to think that carving a turkey is difficult, but it's actually quite simple, as long as you follow these directions. To remove white meat, cut directly downwards until you hit bone, using the breastbone as a guide. Then turn the knife horizontal and cut outwards. Repeat for the other side. You will then have two succulent turkey breasts, which can easily be sliced on a cutting board. To remove legs and wings, pull the appendage away from the body and hunt for the joint with the tip of your knife. When you finally find the cartilage, your knife should be able to cut through it without any problem whatsoever.

Muffin Trick

English muffins are so yummy, and they certainly make a nice change from toast, but sometimes they stick inside the toaster. A great way to rid yourself of this sticky situation is to make an "axle" through the center of the muffin with a toothpick. Place the muffin in the toaster, until it reaches the axle. Toast one half of your muffin "wheel," then pull it out, rotate it around the axle, and then toast the other half. Never, *never*, use anything metal as your axle (see the chapter on safety)!

Easy on the Oil

A lot of today's health conscious recipes call for you to use small amounts of oil when frying, but it can be very difficult (not to mention messy) to measure out the proper amount. You should save your dishwashing detergent bottles once they are empty as they make it simple to dispense small dabs of oil! This really makes it easy to keep your hands and countertops clean when cooking with oil.

Efficient Shopping

If you plan well before going shopping for groceries, then you can cut down both the time and money you spend. First, keep all of the coupons that you collect throughout the week in one place. When you make your grocery list, check it against the coupons you have to see if you can find discounts on what you're going to buy. Second, when writing down your list, visualize to yourself the layout of the grocery store where you usually shop. That way, you can get each item in order from the top of the list to the bottom, without forgetting anything or running back and forth in the supermarket.

Quick Tips

Keep the walls of the kitchen as clear as possible: hanging items translates into more clutter and more clean up work as dust and grease will settle onto these items very quickly.

If you don't have the space for tablecloths, cloth napkins, place mats, towels, etc., hang them from a multi-shirt hanger on the back of the kitchen door.

To increase shelf space, don't be afraid to add extra shelves wherever possible: between two widely separated shelves, in the space between the refrigerator and a wall, underneath a cabinet and above the kitchen counter . . . take a look around your kitchen, the possibilities are endless!

Rolling towels and other cloth items for storage in drawers saves a tremendous amount of space.

You don't have to store all place settings with the same patterns together. For instance, if there are only six members in your family yet you have service for sixteen, place half of your dishes in an out-of-the-way, hard-to-get-to spot.

A circular tie rack can be used to hold small cooking utensils.

Place hooks underneath the shelves of your kitchen cabinets and hang cups, mugs, utensils, small appliances, and other gadgets from them.

Place baby food in a special area (a bread box?) so that they do not get mixed up with the rest of your kitchen foods.

The Bathroom

Like the kitchen, the bathroom is one of the most important rooms in your house. But for some reason, people are almost afraid of cleaning it, as if some scary monster lurks beneath the sink! There are probably dozens of simple things that you can do right now to make your bathroom cleaner, better organized and more efficient. This chapter will instruct you on how to do everything from keeping counter space clean to taking some of the stress out of your morning schedule.

Because the bathroom (along with the kitchen) should be the most sanitary room in your home, it is extremely important to use storage space as efficiently as possible while reducing clutter to a minimum. Unfortunately, because there really is no "furniture" to work with and move around, the bathroom also proves to be one of the most troubling rooms to get organized. But as they say, a little ingenuity can go a long way!

An Organizational Plan of Attack

1) Remove every item in your bathroom, including cosmetics, grooming items, medicinal products, towels, and bath items. You will find these items not only in drawers and cabinets, but on the top of the toilet tank, along the window sill, and around the edges of the bathtub. Go through the products and throw out anything that you don't use anymore. Continue to make a monthly analysis of what you are and what you are not using and discard where appropriate.

2) Clean and line the shelves and drawers with fresh shelf paper.

44

3) Place the products into the following common groupings:

a) Grooming: includes hairbrushes, combs, toothpaste, toothbrush, deodorant, razors, shaving cream, etc.

b) Cosmetics: includes all makeup items, cologne, perfume, after bath powders, oils and creams, etc.

c) Medicinal: includes all prescription medicines, Band-Aids, aspirin, thermometers, cold remedies, etc.

d) Supplies: includes such products as tissue paper, toilet paper, paper cups, and any backup stocks of items from the above categories.

e) Towels: if you still have room in your bathroom, keep a supply of washcloths, hand towels, bath towels, and guest towels in a spare cupboard. If you don't have the room, a nearby linen closet will do just fine.

4) Begin to put away each of the groupings in their own separate area. If space is tight, extra supplies and towels should definitely be stored in other areas of the home. If you must place two groupings together in the same drawer or cabinet, try to keep them separate with the use of a plastic divider or small containers.

Cleaning

Terrific Tracks

I recently polled all of my friends about what they thought was the most difficult part of their bathroom, and they all agreed: the tracks that their shower doors

45

run through. Have you ever peered inside these tracks? It amazes me how much dirt can get caught within them. And when the dirt mixes with the constant barrage of hard water, it turns into a muddy paste. Yuck! I wish I knew an easy way to clean these, but I don't. You're going to have to get on your hands and knees with some bleach and an old toothbrush, and scrub the runners with all your might! Be forewarned that this will get grunge everywhere, so I suggest cleaning the runners before you clean your floor or the bathtub itself. Once you have done this, however, so long as you clean it regularly it will never build up to such a filthy level again (thank heaven!).

Horrible Hair

Hair has a nasty tendency to accumulate around bathroom sinks. Most products have difficulty picking up hair, as static electricity makes it cling to the porcelain. The solution is very simple: Moisten a paper towel and scrub the porcelain. The water will destroy the static charge, and the paper towel will be able to pick up all the hair. Be certain never to flush the towel down the toilet, as it will clog your plumbing.

Unclogging Drains

If your drain ever does become clogged, then I recommend you simply go to the store and buy one of the solutions specifically designed to deal with this problem. They are not very expensive, and they are often far more effective than many of the homemade remedies I have tried in the past. A note of caution: never pour one of these solutions down a clogged toilet, or you will create some very toxic fumes!

Will Do Mildew

Let's face it, most bathrooms are a combination of an extremely humid environment (from all the hot showers you take) and extremely poor circulation (some bathrooms don't have any windows at all). In such a situation, it is impossible for mildew not to grow. But what can you do about keeping it in check? Turpentine is an excellent substance to prevent it from blossoming. Simply soap a sponge with turpentine and scrub the grout in your bathroom. You will have to repeat this every other month. Don't forget to open all the windows when doing this, to insure proper circulation!

Sparkling Sinks

So you really want to clean your sink, but there are so many things sitting on the edge (toothbrushes, combs, razors, etc.) that it looks like too big a chore. Obviously, the solution to this problem is making your bathroom more organized. If you create a set space in your medicine chest or counter to store items like those mentioned above, then your sink will always be free of them. Then, wiping it down is as easy as pie!

Ring Around the Toilet

Forget ring around the collar, what do you do to get rid of ring around the toilet? "Ring around the toilet" is that layer of buildup that occurs right at the water level inside your toilet. This is one of the most difficult things in your home to clean, and it will require considerable elbow grease. Apply an acidic cleanser and scrub. If that doesn't do the trick, then you should try using sandpaper or a moist pumice stone. Be very careful when doing this, however, as some types of porcelain will not accept this kind of cleaning.

Shining Showers

Scientists have been trying for ages to come up with a product that will clean the grime out of showers. Little do they realize that most people already have such a product in their homes. Dishwashing detergent almost always does the trick! You will have to put in considerable elbow grease, but you'll be very surprised by the results.

Fiberglass Wax

Some new homes come equipped with fiberglass showers and bathtubs. If your home comes with such a fixture, then you've probably already come to the conclusion that these are some of the most difficult ones to keep clean. If you don't put any elbow grease into it, then the dirt won't come off. If you do put any elbow grease into it, then you scratch the surface. The best recommendation I can make is to scrub hard and then deal with the scratches. Car wax works well in covering the scratches, although you have to use care in applying it; if you put too much on, then the tub will become slippery and you could fall and hurt yourself. As such, never put any on the floor of the tub!

Soft Faucets

We've all looked down at the faucets in our bathrooms and noticed some stains that seem to have been made by spots of water. But no matter how hard you scrub them, they never seem to go away. These are called hard water deposits, and the key to getting rid of them is to soften the stain. To soften it, pour a small amount of vinegar into a bucket of hot water, and apply the mixture with a sponge. If nothing happens, then slowly increase the concentration of vinegar, until you can rub the stain off. Another method I have used with success in the past is rubbing the stain with a pumice stone. The reason I prefer the first method, however, is that I am always paranoid of scratching the fixtures when using the stone. If you opt to try this second method, you should keep the stone very wet at all times.

Bathtub Blues

Do you have the bathtub blues? You know, that feeling you get when no matter what you try, nothing seems to clean the bathtub well enough? You probably have the same problem with your other porcelain fixtures, such as sinks. You dare not use a scouring powder, as it will probably scratch the porcelain, but soap and water alone do not work well enough. You might want to try mixing your water with a little bit of vinegar. This solution does not work for every type of grime, but it does the trick perfectly for some.

Don't Slip

You know those pretty shaped strips that you put on the floor of your bathtub so you don't slip and hurt yourself? They really can brighten up a bathroom, adding a nice touch that you can enjoy every time you enter. However, they can become discolored very quickly. For a while, I thought the only thing I could do about my dirty strips was to rip them up and replace them with new ones. But I recently learned about this homemade cleanser, and really seems to do the trick: scrub them with turpentine and salt. You'll be delighted with the results!

Ridding Rust

One problem you've probably encountered in your bathrooms dozens of times are rust stains that appear below your faucets on the wall and on the porcelain. These stains might seem impossible to get out, but I have discovered a little trick that I think works quite well. Cut a wedge out of a lemon, put some salt on it (no, you're not making a margarita!), and rub this all over the rust stain. Working together, the salt and the acid from the lemon will cut through the stain. Then use a wet rag to rinse it off.

Soap Scum

If you ask most people what the hardest thing to clean in the bathroom is, then chances are they will say soap scum (you know, that yucky film that builds up on tile walls). You've probably tried just about every kind of cleanser on the market, with inadequate results. The secret is to use a degreaser, as soap scum is actually just a type of grease (if you were a scientist, then you would discover that soap is made of chemicals which mimic the consistency of grease!). Clean small portions of the tiles that are blemished with soap scum, rinsing your sponge off with clean water as you go.

Kitty Litter

Most cat owners keep their litter boxes in their bathrooms, and many complain of the smells they create. Cats are extremely fastidious creatures, and they dislike using a messy litter box. So for their sake and for yours, clean the kitty litter every other day or so. This will prevent a smell from building up, and will let your kitty know you love him enough to care about his comfort.

Cold Disposal

In an economy such as ours, where literally every penny counts, there are all sorts of ways you can find to pinch pennies. Have you ever noticed that when you turn on the water to flush something down the garbage disposal, you probably turn on hot water?

There is no reason to do this. Most people use the garbage disposal at least twice a day, every day. Using cold water for this chore means that you would turn on the hot water at least 730 fewer times each year!

Prevention is the Policy

There are certain steps you can take to prevent your bathroom from becoming a haven for mildew and other problems. First, if you have a window, always keep it open. This will provide enough circulation to help retard the growth of mildew in your grout, which certainly destroys the clean look of your bathroom. Second, make sure there are no leaky faucets or shower heads. Such leaks are the causes of hard water stains and mineral deposits; rather than fighting each stain individually, why not cut them off at the source? Third, use soaps with lower concentrations of fat in them. This will help prevent soap scum from building up in your bathtub. And fourth, clean the shower while you are taking a shower. That way you can kill two birds with one stone!

Fun in the Tub

Bathing your youngster can go much more quickly and smoothly if he or she is entertained. There are all sorts of things you can do to make bath time more fun. Why not save an old egg carton for your child to use as a boat, or add a few soapy bubbles? You can make inexpensive floating toys out of just about anything that you would normally throw out, such as soda bottles. When your child is having fun, he or she won't struggle so much with you, and that way the bath will be completed much more quickly. Additionally, there won't be nearly as much mess to clean up afterwards.

51

Hair Helper

Do you use hair gel or mousse? If so, then take a look at your hairbrush right now. Even if you pull out any tangled pieces of hair (which you should do on a *daily* basis to help prevent build up), the brush probably still looks pretty dirty. Dermatologists warn you not to allow gels and other styling products to build up on our scalps, so why allow them to go unchecked on our hairbrushes? Fill your sink with hot water, add a few drops of shampoo, and dunk the bristles of the brush in the solution for a few minutes, being careful not to wet the handle, which could be damaged by the water. Rinse it off and allow it to dry. You should repeat this procedure at least once a week.

Bathroom Storage

Hanging Baskets

Most bathrooms are small and cluttered, with hardly enough space for one person's belongings, let alone for a whole family's. A good way to solve this problem is to place hooks on the ceiling from which you can hang baskets (much like some flowers are attached to the ceiling) where you can put your toiletries.

Shoe Boxes Aren't Just for Shoes

Remember how you used to keep your favorite toys in shoe boxes when you were a kid? Well, why did you ever stop using shoe boxes for storage? They're sturdy and they come in practical sizes, perfect for holding hairbrushes, combs, spray cans, makeup, toothbrushes and toothpaste. Each member of your family can have his or her own box, and there will never again be any confusion about which item belongs to whom. And as long as you don't lose the lid, then the shoe box can be tucked away almost any-where in the bathroom without dirtying or damaging the things inside.

Make Room for Medicine

Believe it or not, the bathroom is the worst place to keep your medicines. Prescription and nonprescription drugs need to be kept in very stable environments, and the temperature and humidity fluctuates more in the bathroom (due to showers and baths) than in any other room in the house. By putting your medicines in a safe place away from kids in the kitchen or bedroom, then you will clear valuable shelf space for your toiletries.

Handy Loops

For some reason, the people who design bathrooms always seem to forget that children need things placed at lower heights. Young kids very often can't reach towel racks, making it a difficult chore for their parents to clean up after them everyday. Why not buy one of those towel rings, and attach it to the wall at a height that is comfortable for your child?

A Naughty No-No

The worst place in the bathroom to store anything is on the tank of your toilet. Not only is there a serious risk that something will fall into the toilet bowl if you leave the seat up, but it also makes it a difficult chore to open up the tank if you need to adjust the plunger or float bowl inside.

Mirror, Mirror

Most mirrors in bathrooms just aren't big enough for more than one person to look at him or herself at a time. If you find that several of your family members

53

need the mirror at once (for shaving, applying makeup, brushing their hair, etc.) then you should buy a full-length mirror and attach it to the wall horizontally, so that people can stand next to each other. Better yet, to cut down traffic in the bathroom, why not do any personal chores that do not require a sink, such as applying makeup, in the mirror in your bedroom instead? That way, each person will spend less time in the bathroom, and many items, such as hairbrushes, can be stored in bedrooms, thereby increasing counter space.

Sticky Situation

Many medicine cabinets have shelves made out of glass. These shelves can be quite dangerous in two ways. First, their front edges are sometimes extremely sharp. And second, items can be easily knocked from them. If you line the shelves with Styrofoam, then you will rid yourself of both problems. Not only will the sharp edges be covered, but the Styrofoam will also create a considerable amount of friction, "sticking" your items to the shelves.

Tidy Cords

One of the biggest problems with storing things in bathrooms is that power cords from hairdryers and other such appliances get easily tangled. Even worse, these cords can dangle and come into contact with water, which can be very dangerous. To keep your cords neatly wound, and therefore easier to store, simply wind them up and insert them into a used toilet paper tube.

Cotton Dispenser

If you need a place to put your cotton balls, then why not try stuffing them into empty tissue boxes? That way you won't have to hide an ugly plastic bag (the type of packaging in which cotton balls usually come) in your bathroom cabinet, where it will take up valuable space. A tissue box is more than pretty enough to leave in full view.

Secret Hangers

Many people like to hang their clothes to dry from the shower curtain rod, but this can be an unpleasant sight for guests. If you attach several hooks to the inside of your shower curtain, however, then you can hang clothes from these and no one will ever see them! Just make sure to place them high enough on the curtain so that you won't accidentally brush against them and hurt yourself while taking a shower.

Shoe Shine

A good way to keep your bathroom counters shiny and free of clutter is to invest in one of those shoe bags in which 10 or 12 pairs of shoes can fit in their own individual pouch. Shoe bags are very cheap, and you can put just about anything in them, from cans of hair spray to toothbrushes to cleaning supplies. You can even hang them inside doors so that guests won't notice them.

To Each His Own

Most households have more than one bathroom, so why does everyone always wait to get into the same one each morning? Instead of having your family members wait in line, why don't you just keep everyone's toiletries in different bathrooms? That way, since you don't have to wait for each other and organize yourself around each other's schedules, you might be able to get a few more minutes of sleep in the morning!

Bathroom Maintenance and Plumbing

Drip, Drip

While a leaking faucet certainly isn't as complicated to fix as most people believe, here's a neat little idea to rid yourself of the problem for a day or two, before the plumber arrives. Wet a washcloth and squeeze out the excess moisture, so that it is damp but not sopping. Then place the washcloth over the drain where the dripping occurs. This will not solve the problem, but it will get rid of the irritating sound of dripping water. Whenever the washcloth gets saturated with water, simply wring it out and replace it under the leaky faucet.

Dry Porcelain

Don't you hate it when the porcelain fixtures in your bathroom get covered in condensed moisture after you have a hot shower, dripping water all over the floor? Not only can this be a nuisance to dry, but it can also be quite dangerous, as tile floors can become very slippery. In order to minimize this problem, try rubbing some wax on the porcelain at least four times a year.

Clear Mirrors

The mirror in your bathroom always fogs up after you've had a shower, but you can easily solve this by pointing your blow dryer at it and letting the hot air evaporate the moisture. An even better way is to simply drape a towel across it while you bathe. That way, you don't waste any electricity, and the towel is within easy reach.

Clogged Toilets

When a toilet gets clogged, you should usually be able to fix it yourself, saving the high expense of calling a plumber. There are three simple steps to follow. First, scoop some of the water out of the bowl with a bucket. Next, get a plunger and put it as far into the bowl as you can, covering the hole entirely. Pump it vigorously for a few minutes. Repeat every half hour. Finally, if the clog still doesn't come loose, then unwind a toilet snake into the drain and try to pull out the clog. Only after trying these steps should you call a plumber. Never pour any kind of liquid clog remover into a toilet, as a noxious gas could be released.

Clean Shower Heads

Shower heads that are partially obstructed due to a build up of dirt and grime increase your water consumption, as you have to take longer showers to get just as clean. Shower heads are quite simple devices, and they can be removed and taken apart with a few common tools. Place the pieces in an acidic liquid such as vinegar, and leave them overnight. The next day, most of the buildup should be gone, making your shower head more cost efficient.

Clogged Shower Drains

Showers, unlike kitchen sinks, usually tend to get clogged by the same thing over and over again: hair! The following procedure should help you unclog your pipe. Start by pouring a cup of baking soda into the pipe. After a few minutes, add a cup of vinegar. Finally, a few minutes later, add about a half-gallon of very hot (perhaps even boiling) water.

Heavy Curtains

In your bathroom, does your shower curtain seem to get sucked in toward you whenever you turn the water on? This is due to the sudden change in pressure within your shower caused by the force of the water. Try sewing some heavy coins or other small weights into the hem of the curtain.

Soap Dish Mounting

Has your soap dish fallen off the wall long ago, but you just haven't gotten around to fixing it? You should do it as soon as possible, so you can finally remove that bar of soap from the counter around the sink (every bit of storage space counts). Such dishes are very easy to put back on the wall, thanks to the lines of new cements that are now available in hardware stores. You can apply these cements directly to the tiles on your bathroom wall, rather than having to pry the tile off first. Simply follow the directions on the package.

Straight as an Arrow

Some shower heads just don't spray the water in a straight, even line. This can get annoying, as you have to "chase" the water around the tub, wasting precious money (on a needlessly expensive utility bill) and time. If you're not handy with tools, and don't think you can truly fix the problem without calling a plumber, then try this little trick. Cut a hole in the tip of a conical waxed paper cup, and attach the cup to the shower head with a rubber band. The cup will have to be replaced quite frequently, but the water will come out straight. If you can find a more durable item with a small hole in it, such as the top of a soda bottle, then so much the better, as it won't have to be replaced so often. Remember not to turn your water up too high, as the force could dislodge the cup.

Easy Opening

Does your medicine cabinet have two sliding doors in front that overlap each other? You've probably noticed that these doors can get stuck in their runners, and it always seems to happen in the morning when you are late for work. The solution to this problem is simple. Using a cotton swab, simply apply a conservative amount of petroleum jelly to the runners. This technique will also work well with your shower if you have the glass doors that rest in runners.

Sealed Tight

Does it seem like all the grout that should be sealing your bathtub in place is crumbling off? The reason for this is that conventional grout loses its strength over the years when it comes into contact with water. It is an extremely simple job to regrout your bathtub using one of the new high-tech silicone sealants that are available at any hardware store. Simply follow the directions on the tube, and *voila*! Your bathroom will instantly look better.

Dog Bath

If you have a dog, then you know how difficult it can be to bathe one. Not only do they like to jump around, but they leave trails of water and damp hair everywhere. Well here's a little tip to help make your chore a little quicker and easier. In order to prevent your pet's hair from going down the drain, and almost certainly causing a clog, put a piece of steel wool over the drain in place of your usual hair catcher. It will be much more effective!

Quick Tips

Double or triple the amount of space underneath the sink with the addition of one or two shelves.

Nail the bottoms of plastic buckets to the back of the bathroom door and place rolled up towels in the buckets.

Place nails or hooks onto the insides of cabinet doors and hang blow dryers, curling irons, electric razors, and cloth bags which can hold a variety of items—from curlers to barrettes to vitamins!

Place all infrequently used items in the backs of drawers and shelves.

Organize your shower by placing all of your bathing paraphernalia into a shower curtain with pockets or a shower caddy that hangs from the faucet head.

Cut the handle of a plunger in half so that it can be easily stored underneath your sink—it will still work just as well!

The Bedroom

Because the bedroom is the most personal and private room of any household, it should be treated with the utmost care. It is extremely important that, for your own psychological well-being, your bedroom be kept neat and orderly. This is the room where you begin and end each and every day, and so it follows that a clean, bright bedroom will help you attain a more positive self-image and outlook on the world. Additionally, an orderly bedroom will motivate you to keep the rest of your home just as clean and neat.

It has often been pointed out that the average person uses only 25% of his or her clothes on a regular basis. This means that there are most likely a number of items in your clothing collection which can either be discarded or stored in another area of the house. Seasonal items in particular can be stored in an out-of-the-way location until the time of year arrives for their use. Remember that a well-organized clothing collection means that you will get more wear and more exciting combinations out of your clothes, and this will undeniably translate into a healthier and more positive self-image!

An Organizational Plan of Attack

1) Go through your clothes and create a pile out of items you no longer wear because they are out of style, no longer fit you correctly, or are simply worn out. Give this pile to a local charitable organization.

2) Place all out-of-season items into boxes which can be stored elsewhere in your home.

3) Take the clothes which are left over (and hence the clothes that are in the heart of your wardrobe) and divide them into articles which can be put into drawers and items which belong in the closet. Normally all pants, dresses, blouses, shirts, jackets, suits, and sweaters go into the closet while underwear, stockings, socks, pajamas, nightgowns, etc., can be put into drawers. If, however, you have more drawer space than closet space, sweaters, pants, and everyday shirts can exist just fine in a drawer if folded neatly.

4) Divide your closet into everyday wear and evening wear. Then arrange according to type of item, i.e. shirts, pants, blouses, skirts, dresses, jackets, and suits.

5) Organize your drawers in order of how frequently you use each item. For instance, underwear, stockings and socks should go in the most accessible drawer, followed by pajamas and nightgowns, then shirts, pants, sweaters and the like.

Cleaning

Bad Smells!

Bedrooms, as much as we love them, can become havens for bad smells! We spend many hours asleep in our bedrooms, we take off our dirty clothes in bedrooms, and we store our possessions in bedrooms. The best way to prevent bad smells from taking hold is to be conscientious about keeping the room free of them: change your sheets every week, keep your drawers tidy, and take your dirty clothes immediately to the laundry hamper. If a bad smell does start to linger, don't just cover it up with an air freshener, but actually destroy it (and the germs causing it) with a disinfectant.

Dust Destroyers

Dust is a particular problem in rooms with carpeting, such as bedrooms, as pieces of dust can easily become embedded in the carpet fibers. Surprisingly, most people don't know how to dust, and they just waste time and effort. If you are simply dusting with a rag, then the dust will get pushed around, rather than sucked up. Thus, one of the best dusting tools is a vacuum cleaner with a long hose that can reach into nooks and crannies. If you find that you must use a rag, spend the extra money on a rag that is advertised as a dust rag. Such items are treated in the factory with an electric charge, so the particles will stick to them. But when using them, be sure to dust delicately, or the dust particles will still fall off.

Bright Beds

Many people think that taking care of beds is one of the biggest hassles among their household chores. But if you use a little common sense, then you will discover how easy it really is. All that is required is a bit of scheduling. You should wash the sheets *at least* twice a month (once a week is better), and while the sheets are in the wash, take the opportunity to dust the bed frame and turn the mattress. Then simply replace the sheets and you are all done.

Comfy Comforters

Most people have abandoned using quilts as covers for their beds on cold winter nights, and have turned instead to using comforters. These comforters are wonderful to snuggle up to when the temperature is low, but they get dirty very quickly. Most likely, however, your comforter is machine washable. If not, you will have to hand wash it delicately, but even this is easier than the laborious process of cleaning a woven quilt!

64

Water Beds?

Mattresses are some of the most susceptible items in your home; they are almost impossible to clean, and they can virtually be destroyed if you get them wet. So what can you do about this problem, considering you spend one-third of your life atop your mattress? Simple: buy a mattress cover. You can buy such covers in either the waterproof or non-waterproof variety, but I highly recommend the waterproof one, especially if your children are still young. That way you can sleep with ease at night, knowing that nothing will damage your mattress, and the cover can easily be cleaned in the laundry.

Fan-Tastic

If you live in a warm climate, you may have ceiling fans throughout your home, including in the bedrooms. They rarely look dirty, as dust has a tendency simply to fall from their blades. But if you ever remove the blades and inspect the top sides (which you can't see from the ground), then you will be amazed at how much dirt has stuck to them. The best way to handle this problem is simply to soak the blades in warm soapy water for about an hour; the grime will work its way off by itself, and you will rarely need to use any elbow grease at all.

Sneaky Sneakers

Your kid's closet seems to be well organized, and there are no dirty clothes inside, so what could be causing that awful smell? You are not exactly right when you say there aren't any dirty clothes inside; pick up your kid's sneakers and look at the treads. They are filthy, aren't they? With today's new high fashion sneakers (most of which have incredibly deep treads), it's almost impossible to keep the bottoms clean. The solution is simple: don't even bother. Just leave the shoes on the front doorstep. As long as they are kept out of a confined area, such as a closet, they won't smell.

Dusty Plants

Ever since it became common knowledge that plants inhale carbon dioxide and exhale oxygen (photosynthesize), people have been putting plants in more rooms around the house than ever before, including bedrooms. Some doctors feel it is especially healthful for children to sleep in rooms where there are plants providing more oxygen. But plants breathe through the pores on their leaves, and when dust in the room lands on these pores, they can't breathe and will die more quickly. To prevent this from happening, as well as watering the soil that your plants live in, spray their leaves with a misty spray bottle filled with water.

Clutter-Free Nightstand

Keep the tops of nightstands and dressers relatively clear of clutter; this will save you many headaches when it is time to dust. The top of a nightstand should contain only an alarm clock, lamp, and telephone. If you don't have room for a nightstand, place all bedside items—books, a diary, a day-to-day journal, knitting materials, a phone book, a radio, etc.— on a flat dolly that can be easily rolled out from underneath the bed. Just attach a piece of rope to the dolly and tie the other end to the bed's frame. When you want something, simply pull the dolly out from underneath the bed, and when you are through just push the dolly back in place.

Making Your Bed—Adults

Making your bed can be one of the worst chores of the day, but you have to do it each and every morning. But here are a few tips to make it go faster. First, always keep matching top sheets and bottom sheets together, so that you won't have to rifle through the closet looking for them. Second, make marks on each of your bottom sheets, top sheets, and comforters where they meet the four corners of the bed. That way, you can always line up the different layers perfectly. The mark can be sewn on or drawn on. Lastly, if you're in a real hurry, don't be afraid to leave your bed unmade and pat down the comforter neatly over it; you can always make it when you come home from work later in the day.

Making Your Bed—Children

You should definitely teach your kids to start making their beds at a young age, as this will help build their sense of responsibility. But tucking in top sheets and bottom sheets and comforters can be very difficult. That's why a simple quilt can be a better alternative; your kids will learn that making a bed can be quick and easy, and there is no excuse for not doing it.

Personal Possessions

Heavy Handbags

Handbags are like a home away from home; you keep virtually everything you need inside them when you are on the run! But, let's be honest, sometimes you just throw a lot of unnecessary junk inside. You should empty out your handbag at least once a week and throw out all the old gum wrappers and outdated party invitations. As for the outside of handbags or purses, the method for cleaning differs depending on the material out of which it is made. Many cloth bags can actually be cleaned in a tub filled with warm water and laundry detergent, unless a label specifically warns otherwise. Suede and leather bags should be treated with special finishing spray, to help ward off dirt, and you can buy special brushes and cleansers for each.

Jewelry Jubilee

There's nothing so satisfying as being able to dress up for a night on the town and putting on some of your finest jewelry. But if your jewelry is getting dirty or tarnished, then it can completely ruin your fun. I have found that the best way to keep jewelry from tarnishing is by cleaning it regularly, rather than waiting for dirt to build up. Jewelry is too precious to risk on any homemade concoctions, so I just go out and buy a cleanser designed specifically for gems or precious metals. If your jewelry already has a large amount of dirt built up on it, then I suggest you ask a jeweler for advice in cleaning it. You can buy special devices that clean the jewelry by actually shaking the dirt off with sound waves.

Dusty Knickknacks

If you've ever been to a stranger's house, then you've probably tried to find out more about the person by looking at their knickknacks—you know, the little items they have lining their shelves and desks. Does this person have a collection of salt and pepper shakers, or does he have a large number of porcelain figures? As there are so many different types of knickknacks, I can't possibly list all the different ways to clean them. But I can suggest this to you: keep your little knickknacks enclosed in a glass case. Not only will this make them look more valued and treasured, but it will also keep them free of dirt and grime, which means you will have to clean them far less frequently!

Funny Photos

We all have our collection of favorite candid photographs chronicling the best times of our lives. So when one of these photos gets damaged, it is no surprise that this is a heart wrenching incident. Photographs should never get wet, so I highly recommend keeping them in an album which has clear plastic overlays. This will not only prevent any liquid from spilling on them, but it will also keep off any particles of dust. The plastic itself can be easily cleaned with a moist cloth. If you ever do get any liquid on a picture, try to suck it up with a sponge as soon as possible. Once the liquid has penetrated the photographic paper, there is nothing you can do to prevent a permanent mark from appearing. Some people put the negatives to their cherished photos in safety deposit boxes or in a safe if they have one at home, so you might want to consider doing this if you suspect that they might get damaged otherwise.

Super Stereos

If your family is like mine, then one of the most prized possessions in the house is a wonderful sounding stereo. Even though these are highly sophisticated electronic devices, they require very little attention on your part. I highly suggest buying a cabinet for your stereo that has glass doors, so that you can keep the dust out, and you should wipe each component down with a soft dry cloth every week or so, but that is about it. As far as cleaning the sound-producing elements of each component, you will have to buy the appropriate piece of equipment, each of which is very cheap.

You need a head-cleaning tape for your tape recorder, a CD brush for your compact discs, and a record brush for your albums and stylus (if you still own a turntable). Refer to the owner's manuals of each of these items for proper instructions for use.

Computer Cleaning

Almost every household in America now has at least one computer (my household has three!). Computers can be real time savers, allowing you to write letters, balance your checking accounts, and calculate your budget in no time flat. Considering they do so much for you, you should be prepared to keep them clean. First of all, buy some kind of a dust cover to keep dust particles off. I also recommend a rigid cover that fits specifically over your keyboard. You should definitely invest a few dollars in a mouse pad, as this will prevent dirt and grit from getting caught on the ball of your mouse. Whenever you do clean them, the most important tool you should have on hand is a can of compressed air, with which you can literally blow out any dust. Be careful when using such compressed air, however, as the canisters contain a harmful chemical which can be released if used improperly (refer to the directions for use to avoid doing so). I highly recommend against cleaning your computer with even a moist rag, as even a little wetness can do a lot of damage.

Terrific TVs

When you think about all the use we put TVs to, it's quite amazing that they last as long as they do. I have a TV in my house that is over 15 years old, and it still gets as good a picture quality as many of the finest sets you can buy on the market today. Cleaning a TV is remarkably simple. Just dust off the cabinet and controls every week in order to prevent any particles of dirt from entering the electronic components, and clean the screen by rubbing a quilted paper towel across it until you have removed all the grime that builds up due to static electricity. You never need to use any kind of liquid detergent (or even water) when cleaning your TV.

Quick Tips

Use headboards which come with built-in storage shelves, drawers, and night tables.

Hang boots and shoes on skirt hangers—simply attach the tops of the boots and shoes to the two clips on the hanger!

Accordion clothes hangers are wonderful for hanging such items as belts, ties, hats, scarves, gloves and the like.

Keep a tray handy for such items as tie clasps, watches and jewelry. Clear the tray every few days by putting these objects in their proper place.

When sharing a dresser, assign whole drawers to particular individuals rather than sharing parts of a number of drawers.

Build shelves in your closet to hold shoes, sweaters, pants, shirts, and other items.

Suitcases make excellent storage spaces for seasonal clothing.

71

Create an area—either in a corner on a chair or on a "clothes horse" or "clothes valet"—where you can place clothing during times when you just don't feel like putting it away. However, be sure to clear this space on a regular basis.

Place containers (shoe boxes for instance) inside of dresser drawers to separate such items as socks, underwear, stockings, pantyhose, bras, etc.

Use old bathrobes and nightgowns as protective covers for new dresses and suits.

Round oatmeal boxes can be used as hat stands; plus, you can store gloves on the insides of the boxes!

Hang pants on a rod installed on the inside of a closet door.

Place a shoe rack on the floor of the closet to keep your shoes well organized and to utilize what is often neglected and wasted space.

If you have plenty of room for shoes, install a shoe bag on the back of the closet door and use the compartments for belts, stockings, gloves, ties and other accessories.

The metal spine of a three-ring notebook makes a great belt holder—simply remove from the notebook and attach it horizontally to the wall!

If drawer space is tight, bookshelves can be used for storing such items as sweaters, lingerie and underwear. Screen or curtain off the shelves if you wish.

When your children are sharing a closet, paint each side of the closet a different color and paint clothes hangers to match each color in order to help the children keep their respective sides of the closet better organized (this will also help prevent arguments over space).

If you have enough space and money, buying a free standing cabinet can solve many clothes storage problems.

Curtain rods can be used as tie racks.

If you have a particularly high closet ceiling, simply install another dowel near the ceiling. Hang the more infrequently used items in your clothing collection up here, reaching them with the help of a stepladder.

Closets and General Storage

When you clear out and organize your household, there has to be a place for the items which you are keeping, but which are not necessarily kept in view. Obviously, for the most part these items will be placed in the various closets around your home. Therefore, in order to have as much storage space available as possible, it is vital that your closets be meticulously organized rather than a chaotic storage tank for everything and anything.

An Organizational Plan of Attack

1) Begin by assigning every closet in your home a specific function. The closet in your entry hall should be kept free for hanging your guest's coats; the closet near your kitchen and/or dining room should be used for items relating to those two areas of your home; the closet in your den or living room should be used to store photo albums, games, books and other things which you might utilize while sitting in that room. Out of the way closets should be used for storing items like seasonal clothing and nostalgic items which you only take out once in a while.

2) Working on one closet at a time, go through the closets and remove any items that you don't use and which you don't think you will use in the future. Place these objects in a box to give to a charity. Take any item which you want to keep but which belongs in another closet into a box marked with the name of that closet. For instance, if you find toys in the entry hall closet, place these in a box bound for the closet nearest your children's play room. Additionally, don't feel like you must clear out a whole closet all at one

time. Work with individual shelves and areas within the closet, sorting through these smaller spaces at a comfortable pace.

3) Once you have cleared out your first closet, go through your home—including all of the other closets—and remove and return any articles which belong in this first closet.

4) Now that you have only those items which belong in this first closet, organize the closet by placing all items you use most frequently in easily accessible areas, while putting those objects you rarely use in the harder to reach spots in the closet. Additionally, any items which are used together, i.e. sports equipment, cleaning supplies, etc. should be grouped together within the closet.

5) Continue the above process until you have worked through every closet in your home.

Closets

Sticky Situation

Don't you hate it when you're late and trying to rifle through your closet for the outfit you want to wear, but the hangers keep getting stuck on the rod? You can make this problem disappear from your life with a dab of floor wax or furniture polish. When the hangers start sticking again, simply reapply the lubricant.

Smelly Closets

Closets usually smell if they aren't well ventilated. If your closet doesn't have a ventilation duct inside it, then you should leave the doors open overnight (when no guests will be over to see this messy sight). Put some baking soda on the carpet for freshness, and you might even want to tape the wrapper of a scented bar of soap to the wall. Spicy scents are especially good, as they also keep mosquitoes out. It is very important to keep your closet smelling fresh, or your clothes could absorb some foul odors, requiring you to wash them even if you have not worn them.

Wet Closets

Sometimes an undue amount of humidity builds up within your closets, which can ultimately damage your clothing. Such a problem may need to be attended to by a professional, but you can give it a shot yourself. The idea is to fill the closet with dry air. You can accomplish this with either a dehumidifier or, if you don't own one of these, a vacuum cleaner set on reverse.

Rope Trick

Sometimes you just can't find enough space in your closet, no matter how hard you try. Here's a simple way of solving the problem without having to resort to major changes to the closet. Buy a long spool of strong cord. Cut sections of cord from the spool that are about two feet long. Remove all the hangers from your closet. Tie the cord to the neck of one hanger, making the knot just a few inches from the end. You should then have over a foot of cord coming from this hanger. Tie two more hangers to the cord at equal intervals. Then put the top hanger of each set of three back on the rod, allowing the other two to hang down. Once you put all your clothes back on their hangers, your closet will seem only about one-third full!

Clean Closets

There is no great secret to keeping your closet clean. All you have to do is stick to a system of organizing. Many people find that it is best to make themselves a chart listing where everything should go: shirts on the top shelf, pants on the bottom, toys in this corner, shoes in that corner, etc. Then you have to stick to your system. If you spend a few brief moments each day keeping the closet organized, then you'll find that clutter will never have the chance to build up.

Throw it Out

When it comes time for you to organize your (or your children's) closets, you will probably have a hard time because they are so filled with junk. Every household in the world is filled with too much junk. So to clean up this junk, you have to answer one question as realistically as possible: do I really want this anymore? If "this" is something precious or important to you, then naturally you should keep it and find a place for it. But if "this" is that tacky shirt your mother made you wear in the sixth grade, why on earth have you still got it? Throw it out!

Pick the Right Color

The best thing you can do in order to make your closet appear brighter, which is virtually essential for everything to be neat and properly organized, is to paint it the correct color. Most closets are painted white, which is good, but they are usually painted with a matte paint. Repaint the interior of your closet with a glossy paint, and it will seem to shine! If two siblings use a single closet, then why not paint each half a different color in order to help them keep their belongings separate?

79

Closed Curtains

Do you have one of those closets in your bedroom that is so shallow it doesn't even have a closet door? This problem can be rectified by simply hanging a curtain in front of the open closet. Not only will your clothing finally have the privacy it deserves, but you will also have to do laundry less frequently, as dust will not enter the closet so easily.

Create a System

As with your refrigerator, your closet can be a nightmare to keep organized. Why not do yourself a favor and create a system, so that you memorize where everything should go? For example, put all your tops on one side, and all your bottoms on the other. Make sure that your system is sensible; put shoes at the bottom and hats on the top shelf, and not vice versa. In order to help you memorize the locations, make a chart for yourself and tape it to the inside of your closet door. Within a few days, you won't even need the chart anymore.

Home Office Shelves

If you have an empty bedroom that you want to use as a home office, then don't clutter up the floor space by buying a new book shelf. Chances are the closet in the room will be empty, as no clothes will be kept there, so why not turn the closet into a bookcase? Simply add some shelves, and voila!

Soap and Socks

Here are two little tricks to help you out in your closets. First, the best way to hang mothballs in your closet is to put them inside a sock taped to the wall. Second, to keep your clothes smelling fresh and eliminate the smell of mothballs, keep an open bar of soap in the closet. A good alternative to this is to put some cinnamon sticks and bay leaves inside your closet.

Screwy Ties

Tie racks that you find in department stores tend to be quite expensive. Instead of spending your money on such an item, why not build one yourself? All you need to do is take some long wood screws and screw them about a quarter-inch into a piece of wood. Arrange the screws in such a way that they form a nice, straight row. Get a piece of wood long enough to hold about ten screws at intervals of a few inches. When you are done, simply hang your ties from the screws.

Just the Right Height

If you want your child to learn to put on his or her own clothing, then you have to lower the rod so that he or she can reach the hangers. If you're not handy enough to lower the rod, then simply buy another rod (or even a broom handle) and secure it at both ends with strong cords to the original rod, so that the new one dangles below it. Cut the cords to the appropriate length so that your child can reach this rod without having to stretch. Then put all the hangers on this "hanging rod."

General Storage

Useful Luggage

Most people have their suitcases tucked away in the backs of their closets, just wasting precious storage space. They don't want to put their expensive luggage in the garage, basement, or attic, for fear that some rodents might start nibbling on it. You might as well put your suitcase to good use then! Store things inside of it that you don't use everyday. For example, during the summer, why not keep your winter clothes inside it? That way both your suitcases and the clothes within them will be kept perfectly safe.

Keep that Desk Neat

Utensil organizing trays are so useful in the kitchen, so why not use them elsewhere too? They fit perfectly into most desk drawers, and they can easily turn a random pile of odds and ends into a well ordered inventory of supplies. While most adults may be able to keep their home office desks tidy, chores like this are particularly difficult for youngsters, and these trays will certainly help a lot.

Dining Room Desk

If you don't have a room in the house that you can use just as an office, and you don't have the money to move into a bigger house, then why not use the dining room? Dining room tables are often bigger than most of the desks you can buy at office supply stores. Instead of buying filing cabinets, just put your paperwork in the drawers and shelves of your cutlery holders. That way, no one will ever know that your dining room is doubling as an office.

Organizational Plan of Attack—Books

1) Remove your books from the bookshelves and wipe down the shelves and the books, getting rid of all dust and dirt.

2) Sort through the books and place all damaged and out-of-date material in a carton to be given away to a

charity. You should also look carefully at any textbooks, which often have not even been opened since those good old school days.

3) Take any books which you would like to keep but which don't necessarily have to be kept on the bookshelf, i.e. nostalgic items or collector's editions, and pack them into a carton. Clearly identify the carton with a black marker that specifies which authors and/or titles the carton holds.

4) Arrange the remaining books by subject (Art, Sports, Travel, etc.), and then arrange them alphabetically by author within each subject heading. Have one section for particularly large and/or oversized books.

5) Place the books back on the shelves, with the most commonly used books (reference books, for example) in the most accessible areas.

Organizational Plan of Attack—Files

1) Create a designated office area where all paperwork is to be handled. In the area, you should keep such filing supplies as file folders, labels, and a ball point pen. Your paper, cardboard, or metal filing cabinet should also be located nearby.

2) Divide all paperwork into three initial categories: "To be filed," "Things to do," and "Things to throw away." Immediately place all of the items that are in the "Things to throw away" pile in a trash can.

3) Take the "To be filed" pile and divide up the material into individual categories. Common designations include, "automobile," "credit cards," "telephone," "newspaper clippings," "letters," etc. If your file folders do not include one of your divisions, then create a new file, complete with a new label, filled out with a ball point pen.

4) If you have a large amount of material to file within any particular category, consider setting up a filing system which uses subdivisions. For instance, under the category "automobile," you could have such subdivisions as "gasoline expenses," "car insurance" (although you might want this to go under the "insurance" heading), "receipts for mechanical expenses," "new car literature," "registration material," etc. Keep a separate file folder for each of these subdivisions within, or in back of, the larger folder titled "automobile." If you clip and save a fair amount of newspaper clippings, instead of placing them all in one folder under "newspaper clippings," consider placing them in subdivisions according to the subject of the article, for instance "sports," "travel," "politics," etc. You can even create subdivisions within these smaller categories, for example "basketball," "football," and "baseball" underneath the subdivision "sports."

5) Divide the "Things to do" pile into smaller categories such as "bills to pay," "R.S.V.P.'s to make," "things to discuss with my husband," etc. All aspects of a particular project should always be kept together. For example, if you are buying a new car, then all prices, literature, phone numbers of car salesman, etc. should be kept in the same file together.

6) Keep a "To do" box or file and a "To file" box or file in an easily accessible location within your office area. Whenever you get mail or any other kind of paperwork that needs immediate attention but you cannot get to the job right away, place the material into one of these two boxes or files.

Quick Tips

Always put empty hangers in the same place on the rod (not the same place where the item of clothing was found), so that you always know where to find them. Also, always place hangers on the rod so that the hooks face the back wall of the closet. That way you won't have to struggle to remove them.

Keep a flashlight in closets where there is no light bulb.

Installing adjustable shelves, free standing storage units complete with drawers, and hooks attached to walls and the inside of doors helps to increase the storage space within closets.

Sore one extra set of sheets and pillow cases underneath each mattress in the home, and place all leftover linens in boxes which can be efficiently stored in an out-of-the-way place. This will free up so-called "linen closets" for other uses.

Utilize the upper areas of closets by attaching shelves, rods and/or dowels to the walls and using a step ladder to get to the infrequently used items which are stored there.

To save valuable floor space, hang items like bicycles and vacuums which you would not normally think of hanging.

To give yourself more room on your bookshelves, place all cookbooks on a shelf in the kitchen, all art books in the art studio (if you have one), all children's books in the children's room, and even a few pleasure-reading books in a guest room so that your visitors will have something to read.

Place an extra shelf in the middle of a high shelf area to create two shelves and a lot more space!
Shelve paperback books in a double layer, leaving the front row loose enough so that the back row is easily accessible.

Keep extra room available on your bookshelves for any books you may buy in the future. If you file your books so tight that there is no room for expansion, you will soon be faced with disorganized shelves once again.

Be ruthless in throwing away old paperwork that has no use or meaning to you any longer. Old bills, receipts, clippings, out-of-date warranties, etc., are just a few of the many types of paper clutter that jams up files and office areas.

Keep coupons in a separate recipe box organizer, divided according to either the type of product or the name of the store.

Do not keep newspapers that are more than a day or two old inside of your home. Old stacks of newspapers are ugly, dusty and create a cluttered atmosphere.

Build shelves along the walls of the garage to store everything from small items such as screws and nails to larger items like hibachis and sports equipment.

Place an old cabinet, dresser or cabinet in the garage to store equipment and supplies.

Nail two by fours across the exposed studs along the walls of the garage and store tall, thin items like lumber, rakes and shovels behind them.

Furniture, Walls, Floors, Windows, Drapes and Doors

When it comes down to it, our home, however lovely it may be, is really just one big storage chest for our furniture. So you can't clean your home without cleaning your furniture. But furniture can be extremely tricky to keep neat, so this chapter has been written with that in mind. This chapter will offer hints I have learned throughout the years to get stains, nicks, and burns out of my favorite pieces of furniture, and even to prevent such atrocities from occurring in the first place.

I will also be looking at walls and floors in this chapter. Speaking of which, when *was* the last time you took a really good look at your walls? You would be amazed at how greasy and dirty they can get. Go over to them right now, and inspect them closely, in a spot where there is a lot of light. Yuck! How can so much dirt build up on a wall? Where does it all come from? Now take a look at the floor directly under where you are sitting or standing. You will probably be shocked at how dirty it is. Just look at the treads of your shoes, and you'll get a good idea as to why it is this way. This chapter will not only cover how to go about cleaning walls and floors, but it will also discuss strategies for preventing the dirt from settling on these surfaces in the first place!

Finally, windows and doors are our sole connections with the outside world when we are inside our homes. If you stop to think about how often they are used each day, about how many different pairs of hands touch them every single day of the year, it suddenly becomes easy to understand why they are always so dirty. Windows are especially problematic, as they are made of glass; sometimes glass seems to have been invented for no other reason than to make dirt and grime noticeable! Windows also sometimes get left open during inclement weather, which means the pane, the sill, and even the curtain or drape will all get dirty from the rain. This chapter will give you plenty of hints and tips on dealing with these particularly difficult areas of your home.

Furniture
Plenty of Polish
Polish truly does make furniture look healthier and younger. However, polish does nothing to preserve the wood. It doesn't necessarily damage the wood per se, but it does simply create another coating that will need to be removed when it comes time to strip the wood and revarnish it. As such, you should polish as rarely as possible. If you are careful with your wooden furniture, then you should rarely need to resort to polish, as opposed to simply wiping it down with a damp cloth.

Luxurious Leather
So you've just bought a luxurious new leather couch, but you're not sure how to take care of it. First of all, don't clean it *too* often. Second, go out and buy a special type of soap known as saddle soap (this is not a brand name, but a product name). The saddle soap must be mixed with water and rubbed over the furniture until a huge amount of suds has been formed. The saddle soap you buy will have specific directions for the proportions of water and soap that should be mixed, etc. Saddle soap is different from other soaps because it actually makes leather younger, removing brittleness and restoring its original suppleness. Please

91

note that saddle soap cannot be used with certain types of leathers, so read the directions closely.

Cigarette Sorrows

We've all known the agony of seeing our finest sofa forever destroyed by a cigarette burn. There are ways to help alleviate the damage of a burn to your upholstery, but they can be far too complex for the scope of this book. But burns are not the only damage that cigarette smoking can do to your furniture. The smoke produced by cigars and cigarettes can create a thick layer of residue on your furniture, dulling its finish. For wooden furniture, I suggest dusting frequently, and you will probably find that you have to polish more frequently if someone in your home smokes. For upholstered furniture, you will have to dry clean it at least twice a year, which will even destroy the scent. For either type of furniture, the best solution is the most simple: only smoke when you are outside!

Gorgeous Glass

Glass tables are so beautiful, but they are easily blemished by finger prints. If you have a glass table at home, then you know how hard it is to clean it without leaving streaks or smudges. The best way to clean these tabletops is to moisten them with a mixture of water and a few drops of vinegar. Rather than using a rag, you should loosely crumple up some newspaper and rub the table clean with it. If the finger prints remain, then increase the amount of vinegar and repeat this process.

Pushin' Cushions

The bottoms of the cushions in your couch can be scary things to look at, but you must clean them every so often. The top will generally be quite clean, as you probably vacuum them, but the undersides will be horrid! Think about everything that has fallen out of people's pockets and gotten stuck there. Here's a good routine that will ensure the cleanliness of your cushions. Once a week, turn them over. There's no real top or bottom to a cushion (although there is a back and a front, as defined by the location of the zipper). By turning them over, you will be able to keep both sides clean, and you will prevent one side from getting excessively worn.

Gleaming Grills

If your barbecue grill is only somewhat dirty, with a little carbon scoring on it, then you might simply turn it on and heat the grill up. Once it gets hot, simply scrape the residue off with a grill scraper. If this doesn't work, then submerge it in a bucket of warm soapy water for a day or two, and then try re-scraping. If this still doesn't work, then you should consider investing in a new stainless steel grill, which can be cleaned with oven cleaner.

Wooden Worries

Due to its relatively low cost, unfinished wood furniture is becoming more popular every day. Such unfinished wood furniture is available in beautiful designs and varieties, for far cheaper than similarly finished furniture costs. But, many people think that it is okay to bring the furniture home and leave it as is. This couldn't be further from the truth! Wood is a porous material, and dirt literally gets trapped inside. You must finish the wood in some way, either with varnish or paint, in order to be able to keep it clean. Then you can handle it just like any other furniture (polishing only when necessary).

Wonderful Wicker

Wicker furniture is a great way to add some spice to your home, whether you put it inside or out. But as it is such functional furniture, it often gets dirty. For general cleaning, you should vacuum it once a week with the hose of your vacuum cleaner. Wicker can be washed, but you have to dry it in a very controlled manner or it will shrink and lose its shape. If you do decide to clean it with water, never use any harsh cleansers on it (read the label for an indication of gentleness, or you could even try using a small dash of dishwashing detergent), and keep a highly absorbent towel on hand to soak up as much of the water as possible.

Inside Out

When removing a stain from cloth upholstery, the best advice is to try removing it from behind. In other words, if you are trying to get a stain out of a couch cushion, then remove the upholstery from the cushion and turn it inside out. Then test several types of cleansers on the stain. Some will naturally work better than others, and some might actually damage the upholstery. That is why you have turned it inside out. If you damage it slightly, no one will notice, because they will never see this side!

Magic Powder

It is always best to get to a spill before it sets and becomes a stain. If you ever spill a drink on a piece of upholstery, as in the entry above, then attend to it immediately. Use a paper towel like a sponge, allowing it to soak up the liquid delicately; in other words, don't lean all your weight on it in hopes of it absorbing faster, because you will just force the liquid deeper into the upholstery. When the spill is mostly gone, sprinkle enough talcum powder over it to cover the area of the spill. Talcum powder acts like a sponge, sucking up the moisture. After a few minutes, vacuum it off. If there is any moisture left, repeat this until it is gone.

Gum Gripes

If you have kids, then chances are you've found a piece of hard gum stuck under one of your tables, chairs, or couches. The gum has often solidified to the point where it cannot be removed with a knife, because the knife simply bends under the pressure. But try scraping it off with a quarter. You'd be amazed how tough these coins are! Once the lump of gum is removed, if the residue is in a place where it cannot be seen or will not attract too much dust, then you can probably just leave it there.

Lots of Light

Keep all of your lamp shades and lights well cleaned. You'd be amazed at how much light a layer of dust can prevent from escaping a bulb. Many people find that by keeping their lamps free of dirt, they can often install bulbs that use an average of 10 to 20 watts less than the previous bulbs they replaced! Over the course of the year, this will mean tremendous savings on your electricity bill. Incidentally, while we are on the subject of saving money, always clean during the day, so you won't have to turn on extra lights in order to find the dirt.

Globe Waters

Due to the kind of static electricity generated by light bulbs, the glass globes that cover many ceiling lights attract inordinate amounts of dust. You'll probably find that dusting alone will not allow you to get rid of this dirt and grime. Carefully remove the globe (never stand on a ladder without someone holding it for support, and always wait until the light has cooled down!). Fill a bucket with warm water and a few drops of soap (dishwashing detergent works well), and dunk the light fixture into this solution. With a clean sponge, rub the globe until all the dirt has come off. Always make sure it is perfectly dry before replacing it on the light, or you run the risk of electric shock!

Family Fireplace

If you live in a state where the weather gets cold, then you probably know the wonderful feeling that can only be attained by sitting around a warm fireplace with your family. The only problem is that the next day, when you look at the fireplace, you notice that the bricks are covered with plenty of black soot and stains! These kind of stains can immediately give the whole room dingy, as the fireplace is often the focal point of one's attention when entering a room. But these stains can be cleaned by drenching them in cola, and then scrubbing away with a stiff brush doused in hot water. It is interesting to contemplate the kind of damage colas must do to your teeth if they are strong enough to remove soot from a brick!

Terrific Toothpaste

Toothpaste!? Why am I talking about toothpaste in a book of helpful household hints? Well, it turns out that toothpaste is an excellent way to cover up small blemishes in wooden furniture. Dab a little bit of tooth paste on the blemish (only use *paste*, not gel!). Rub it into the wood, wiping with the grain (as opposed to across it). Then buff it off with a clean rag. *Voila*! No more blemish.

Perfect Plastic

Because pre-assembled furniture is so expensive, pressed wood furniture is becoming more common every day. This is the kind of furniture that you buy in a box and assemble at home. It is generally coated with a layer of plastic that is textured and painted to look like wood. This kind of plastic coating smudges easily, and store bought cleansers are generally too harsh on it. Warm water mixed with a few dashes of dishwashing detergent generally does the trick, however, and smudges can be removed with just a little bit of elbow grease.

Shining Chandeliers

Chandeliers are beautiful fixtures that add a certain amount of elegance and class to any dining room or living room. But by virtue of the fact that they are so ornate, they can be extremely difficult to keep clean. The best cleansers I have found are the special detergents made for chandeliers; this is not simply because of the detergents themselves, but also because of the spray dispensers in which they come. Lay some kind of tarpaulin on the ground beneath the chandelier, spray it with the detergent, and watch the dirt and grime just fall to the floor. It is advisable to do this during the daytime, so that you will be able to see with the chandelier turned off (to reduce the risk of shock, no lighting fixture should ever be illuminated while you are cleaning it!).

Precious Pianos

Pianos are one of the only types of musical instruments that also truly qualify as pieces of furniture. In fact, a piano is often one of the most elegant pieces of furniture in a home. So if you make the expensive investment of buying a piano, then you owe it to yourself to keep it looking, as well as sounding, beautiful. The wood should be cleaned just as any other wooden piece of furniture: remove dust frequently with a soft cloth, wax only when necessary, etc. But the part that gets dirty most quickly is, naturally, the keyboard (in most households it is the children who play the piano, and they don't seem to understand the harm in playing with their hands covered in grime!). The keys should be cleaned with a soft cloth that has been dipped in toothpaste or plain yogurt!

Sparkling Silver

Many pieces of furniture are accented or detailed with fine metals. My mother, for example, is still in possession of her father's prized writing desk, which has silver knobs on the drawers. Even if you don't have any such furniture, then the following tips will help you clean the silverware you have at home. First of all, if you can do so without damaging the furniture in any way, then I highly recommend removing the silver accent so it can be cleaned separately. I wouldn't do this too often; no more than once or twice a year, or you seriously increase the risk of causing some damage. I have never used the polishes that you actually dip silver into, but I have been told they are extremely harsh and can cause considerable deterioration. I suggest using a fine silver polish and a soft cloth, and remember that you barely need to put any pressure on the accent when you are rubbing or buffing.

Scratch Magic

If your wood furniture has any scratches on it, then I highly suggest trying to fix it without using polish (as already discussed, buildups of polish can be very bad for your furniture). If the scratch in the furniture is quite deep, then apply some shoe polish to it that is the same color as the wood. Apply as little as possible, and buff it in well. But if the scratch is light, then you can get away with using, of all things, a walnut! Crack open the shell, and rub the nut itself over the gouge. Nuts are very oily, and the oil will fill in the small gap.

Rust Away

If you have any iron furniture in your home or in your yard, then you've probably noticed that it rusts extremely easily. Unfortunately, when it comes to this kind of corrosion, there is no magic cure-all. You will probably have to sand off the rusty areas, repaint the furniture, and then cover it with some kind of varnish. To prevent it from getting rusty in the first place, you should dust it every day and keep it away from moisture as much as possible (yes, if you keep your iron furniture outdoors, that means taking it inside when it rains).

Bandage Blues

No one knows exactly how it happens, but if you have children, then you are bound to find an old adhesive bandage stuck to one of your cushy pieces of furniture! The glue on these bandages is quite strong, but don't worry, because you can usually remove it without damaging the furniture. First, very carefully peel the bandage off. It is better to have some glue left on the furniture than it is to pull off some of the fabric. Then, using tweezers, pluck off as much of the residue as you can. Be patient, because to do this right can take considerable time. Finally, use a special kind of detergent known as a dry spotter to remove the tiny remainder of the residue. This is a special chemical, akin to what is used in dry cleaning, so you should follow the directions closely in order to utilize it effectively and safely.

High Chair Hijinks

If the high chair you have bought for your baby is made out of plastic, then here's a neat little trick for keeping it clean (I bet you've been waiting for this one, especially if the youngsters in your house make as much of a mess as they do in mine!): take it into the back yard and spray it down with your garden hose. I know this may seem extreme, but the water pressure, more than anything else, will actually blow the food particles off the piece of furniture. You should also take out a sponge and wipe it down with a little soap, being sure to rinse it thoroughly. Don't you wish it were so easy to clean your baby as well?

Drawers that Stick

If your desk drawers are getting stuck, then you probably have to force them open with all your might. This destroys all of your attempts at being organized, as everything within the drawer slops around. To solve this problem, remove the drawer. Take a piece of coarse sandpaper (sandpaper comes in varying grades, from coarse to fine) and sand down the sides of the drawer a bit. Then take some floor wax and work it into the bottom. Be careful not to use too much, however, or one tug will make your drawer fly right out of the desk.

Less Scratchy

If you have an office at home where you greet clients or associates, then your office furniture must look very respectable. To remove small scratches from fine wood desks and chairs, mix together a teaspoon of mineral oil and a tablespoon of mashed pecans. Apply the mixture to the scratch, and buff until the scratch is no longer noticeable. This will not eliminate larger and deeper scratches, but it does make them more difficult to see.

Makeshift Furniture

When we were young, we always used to look for creative solutions to a problem, so why don't we do that anymore? If you don't have enough money to furnish your office with "real" furniture from an office supply store, then why not make some yourself? Sturdy cardboard boxes make excellent filing cabinets, for example. Simply divide the boxes into sections for each letter of the alphabet using appropriately marked pieces of paper, and slide your files in! While a desk can't be made out of cardboard, it can be made from cinder blocks and wood. You won't even need any real assembly to build your desk, either; simply stack the bricks up to the correct height (I suggest making a solid leg on either side, rather than a pedestal at each corner) and lay the plank of wood on top. Your desk will probably cost less than twenty dollars!

Walls and Floors

Think First

One of the best ways for you to save time when cleaning floors is to be able to hide any dirtiness. Thus, if you are buying new flooring (be it carpet or linoleum), or if you are planning on moving into a new home, then here are a few suggestions: First, think about the color. Black and/or white will reveal any dust, whereas intermediate colors like brown will hide it. Then, think about the texture. When buying a linoleum floor, a ridged floor is very difficult to keep clean as the dirt has so many nooks and crannies in which to get trapped.

Magic Mat

Have you ever noticed that the floor near the bathtub seems to have more mildew growing on it than anywhere else in the bathroom? The reason for this is quite simple: water from baths and showers slops out over the edge of the tub, drips into the grout, and causes mildew to form. The solution to this problem is equally simple: bunch the bath mat up so close to the tub that any excess water hits it instead of the floor! This is an example of "preventative cleaning."

Dusty Walls

One of the easiest ways to keep your walls clean is by preventing them from getting dirty in the first place. And the reason they get dirty is because of the amount of dust in the air! Don't get offended, because dust is present in the air of everyone's house, no matter how often you clean (in fact, one of the most common types of dust particles are dead skin cells!). So do whatever you can to decrease the amount of dust in your home: vacuum more frequently, check the air filters in your air conditioner, etc.

Fine Filter

As indicated by the entry above, a dust filter is one of the best ways to keep your walls clean. Dust filters are not extremely expensive, so I suggest that you consider investing in one. If your home is already equipped with a central air conditioner, then it can very easily and inexpensively be adapted to be an air filter. And here's an extra way to ensure the cleanliness of the air that comes through the filter: attach a piece of cheese cloth to the grill. Cheese cloth is porous enough to let air through, but the pores are small enough to filter out even the smallest pieces of dust.

Radiant Rugs

Many people have rugs placed throughout their homes in order to keep rooms looking bright and colorful. But that effect is ruined once the rug starts to get dirty. How can you solve this problem? Simply soak it in a solution of cold water and vinegar. It is best to hang-dry a rug, but tossing it into a dryer (just be sure to read the care instructions for your particular rug) is normally a safe alternative.

Shoe Scuffs

Black scuff marks are hardly appealing, and they can be quite a chore to clean up. If you have to deal with such scuffs, then there are two different procedures, depending on whether you have a waxed or no-wax floor. For waxed floors, clean with a solution of vinegar and warm water; anything stronger than this is likely to eat through the wax. For no-wax floors, use a chemical known as dry spotter, which is similar to what dry cleaners use (as with any chemical, read the directions carefully in order to use it safely and effectively).

Gooey Gum

If you have kids in your household, then you've probably encountered gum stuck to your beautiful carpet! This situation may seem horrible at first, but it is actually not that difficult to clean up. The secret is to make the gum as cold as possible. That way it will solidify and contract. Simply rub it with an ice cube for a few minutes, and then you can easily scratch it off.

Correct Cork

Cork is becoming a common type of flooring, due to its cost efficiency relative to other types of floors, and due to the fact that it never creaks. But cork can be very burdensome to clean up, as dirt particles fall so easily into the air pockets. The best way to keep a cork floor looking new is to vacuum it regularly, sucking the dirt out. You should wash it very occasionally with water into which you have added some lemon or vinegar. If these techniques don't work for you, then you might want to apply a layer of wax on top and then treat it like any other waxed floor.

Blood Blots

Blood is, without a doubt, one of the most difficult substances to get out of any carpet. The stain it creates, if allowed to settle in, might never be removed, so you have to clean it as soon as you can. This method doesn't always work (with blood, no method does), but I have found that it usually does the trick. Douse a rag with the most powerful store bought cleanser you have, and scrub it into the stain with all your might. Then rub a bit of shaving cream into the spot. Follow this with a mixture of water and vinegar. Finally, when the water has dried, run the vacuum cleaner over it. If the stain hasn't disappeared by this time, then rest assured that you have done the best you can.

Smoking Smudges

If you've ever wondered why your walls always seem to look so dull and smudgy, even though you have no children to rub messy hands all over them, then perhaps I have the answer: if you, or anyone in your home, smokes cigarettes, then the smoke will create a thin layer of "dullness" that will eventually coat all of your walls. The best way to prevent this is not to smoke, or at the very least smoke only outdoors. Cleaning up this dullness isn't very hard, but it is time consuming, as you have to wash every wall! Simply mix a solution of water and cleanser and start scrubbing (be sure to test the solution to make sure that it is not too harsh for your brand of paint). If you still notice the smell of the tobacco, then chances are it is trapped in the fibers of your carpet; follow the directions for deodorizing your carpet elsewhere in this chapter.

Edge Attacks

Vacuum cleaners just aren't made in such a way that it is easy to get to the edges of floors. In fact, if you're like me, you sometimes just "attack" the edges out of frustration, and all that ends up happening is you bash the vacuum cleaner into the wall. The solution to this problem is simple: there is no problem! People very rarely walk right in the edge of rooms, so they don't get too dirty. If you do notice some dirt, simply sweep it up.

Half Full?

Here's a great way to keep your electrical bill as low as possible when vacuuming. Rather than waiting until the bag in the vacuum is all the way full, empty it out at the halfway point. You see, when a bag gets more than half full, the vacuum has to work extra hard to suck up dirt. This can affect the amount you spend on your utility bill!

Magic Carpet

Right now, in your home, you have a magic carpet. No, I don't mean one that flies! But this has happened to me dozens of times, and I bet it's happened to you:

I have cleaned a spot from a rug, being careful not to damage the carpet fibers, but a short while later the stain is back! This is actually not magic, but a genuine scientific phenomenon with one of those long names I was never able to remember. You see, if you don't remove the stain altogether (if some of it remains at the bottom of the carpet fibers), then when the water that you applied to the surface of the carpet dries, the stain actually climbs the carpet fibers! I wish I could explain it in better detail, but I don't understand the process very well myself. All you need to know is that you should be sure a stain is removed entirely, or else don't be surprised if it "magically" comes back to haunt you.

Linoleum?

The floor in your kitchen is probably linoleum, right? Wrong! Everyone refers to just about every type of kitchen floor as linoleum. But real linoleum hasn't been common for many years, because it is a difficult material to keep clean. If you are certain that you have a true linoleum floor, there are a few things you can do to make your chores easier. First, put down a coating of wood sealer over it. Then wax it regularly with a wooden floor wax. If you follow these directions, you should be able to handle any day-to-day dirt with no trouble at all.

Mighty Masonry

Masonry flooring, that is flooring made of some kind of brick or baked clay, is one of the most beautiful ways you can finish your home. These floors look appropriate both inside and out, but considering their tough appearance, they are surprisingly susceptible to damage. As such, your first chore in dealing with them should be to finish them with a sealer designed specifically for masonry. Please note that there are different finishes depending on whether the masonry is in your home or outside, and you have a choice between a matte or a gloss finish. You will be delighted at how easy it is to keep these floors clean after having put in this simple effort.

Magic Mark Remover

Another problem encountered by households with children is crayon markings on linoleum floors (kids love to play in the kitchen when their parents are around). The magic ingredient to make such stains disappear is silver polish. This polish will also remove the top layer of wax, however, so you will have to re-apply a coating.

Mighty Mats

Most homes have a mat outside their front door (you know, the traditional "welcome" mat). But here's an idea to make your mat even more effective. Put a second mat inside your front door. Even if your guests are courteous and polite, chances are they will not get all the dirt off their shoes by wiping them on the outside mat. By letting them walk on the inside mat before actually coming into contact with carpet or flooring, you will decrease the amount of dirt in your home considerably.

Finished Floors

Finished floors are the easiest ones to keep clean. They have a permanent layer of varnish on them, which allows them to be cleaned very efficiently with soap and water. Many different types of floors can be finished, but it is most common to finish wooden floors. Even if you use the mat technique as described in the previous entry, I suggest that you finish the floors in rooms that lead outside. That way, if anyone tracks any dirt in, you can clean it up very easily. To get instructions for finishing your floor, go to a local hardware store and ask for assistance.

Perfect Paint

If you've ever tried to remove a stain from the wall, then you've probably noticed that many store-bought cleansers can damage the paint, dulling its luster or discoloring it altogether. A homemade trick you can try is scrubbing the stained wall with a mixture of warm water and vinegar. Vary the concentration of the solution according to the difficulty of the stain. For tough stains, use more vinegar, for simpler ones, use less. If your wall is painted with flat paint, then you have to be extra careful, as they can be damaged most easily; in other words, use as little vinegar as possible. Another hint to keep in mind is that you should always start from the top and work your way down.

Steam Cleaning?

We have all looked at our carpets and said to ourselves, "These are so dirty that they have to be steam cleaned." If your carpet hasn't been steam cleaned in a few years, then now is definitely the time to do so. I recommend simply renting a steam cleaning machine from a supermarket, as they are so inexpensive. But if you would rather leave it to the professionals, then I suggest waiting until the next batch of coupons comes in the mail. You've probably noticed that most coupon books seem to include deals on carpet cleaning. You should not steam clean too often, or you will bog down the fibers with moisture, and eventually wear them away altogether. But you should deep clean it in such a way at least once a year. By doing so, you will notice that your regular vacuuming seems to yield much better results.

Clean Carpets

New carpeting is one of the best ways of making your home look fresh and brand new. Ironically, in trying to maintain the luster of new carpeting, many people actually destroy it! Simply put, don't wash your carpet until it is absolutely necessary, or you will remove the chemical coating with which it is treated.

Terrible Tar

Without a doubt, one of the most difficult substances to remove from your carpet is tar! If someone in your family is involved in the construction business, or if you have ever had any construction done on your house, then you know how easily tar sticks to the soles of someone's shoes, and then gets transferred to your carpet. To remove the tar stain, scratch off as much as you can with a spoon. Then, take a piece of steel wool and drench it with white toothpaste (I stress paste, rather than gel). It will take a considerable amount of elbow grease, but the paste and the steel wool should be able to get rid of most of the stain.

Wall Vacuum

If you inspect your wallpaper closely, you will probably notice that it has many grooves in it from where the fibers from the paper are interlaced. The reason wallpaper seems to dull so quickly is that dirt gets trapped in these grooves. In order to prevent this from happening, you might want to try vacuuming your wallpaper! Once the larger particles of dirt have been removed, you can then scrub out the remainder with a damp sponge.

Messy Marble

Marble is one of the most beautiful ways you can finish a home (just think about all those luxurious European estates and castles!), but it is far too expensive to be accessible to most people. Accordingly, many homes now come with walls and sinks finished in "cultured marble," or a surface that emulates the look of marble. This type of surface doesn't stain very easily, but it is delicate and reacts poorly to cleansers. Some detergents literally eat through the surface like acid! So, if your home has cultured marble in it, then I suggest testing a variety of cleansers in an inconspicuous spot to see which ones work the best.

Carpet Trouble

Carpets can become a nightmare when something is spilled on them because there are so many tiny crevices into which the spill can run. The first rule to remember is that you should clean it up as soon as possible; this will increase your chances dramatically of preventing a stain from setting in. If you spill a drink or other liquid, then try to suck up as much of it as possible with paper towels (for some reason, sponges don't work very well on carpets). Once you have soaked it up, you should apply a small amount of soda water. The clear fizzy liquid will help push any last drops of the spill to the surface.

Waxing Wood

Wood floors are one of the most beautiful aspects of any household. They add a certain amount of elegance and class to a room, and they go with virtually any type of furniture, a quality which many carpets cannot claim! But wood floors are difficult to keep clean, requiring a good scrubbing with soap and warm water, followed by an application of wax (often by hand). If you happen to have a bit of extra money in the bank, you might want to consult with an expert about applying a no-wax coating. Then your wood floor will be as easy to clean as any no-wax floor.

Too Much Wax?

I know that this might sound irritating after just having read the previous entry about the need to wax wooden floors, but you will soon learn that housekeeping is a matter of keeping things in balance. Too much wax is just as bad as not enough! If you think that your floor has too much wax on it, then go to an unused corner of the room and scrape with a razor blade. If no wax comes off, then your floor does not have too much wax, and the small scratch you might have created will go unnoticed. If a substantial amount of wax comes off, then you have wax build up and must remove it. Go to a hardware store and buy a wax removing chemical. Read the instructions to this chemical carefully, as they can create very toxic fumes. Once your floor is stripped of wax, then you can reapply a new coat.

Rubber Helper

Many modern kitchens are following in the footsteps of the kind of industrial kitchens found in restaurants and hotels by having rubber flooring installed, to make clean up easier. But if you are not careful, you can damage your rubber floor very easily when cleaning it. Chemicals, such as the kinds found in soap, can actually eat through your beautiful rubber floor. The best way to keep it clean is to sweep it everyday, and to mop it with warm water mixed with lemon or vinegar every two or three days.

Practical Dust Pan

Let's face it, most dust pans you can buy are complete wastes of money. Their lips are so thick that you can never get all of the dust off the floor and into the pan! You'll find that when it comes to keeping your home neat and tidy, ingenuity is the most important trait you can have. An ingenious little substitute that you can use for a dust pan is the thin piece of cardboard that comes as the backing to a new men's dress shirt. This kind of cardboard is thin enough, but it is also amazingly tough, which means it probably won't wear out before you have bought another shirt and can replace it.

Sanding Cigarettes

If you've ever thrown a party, then chances are one of your friends who smokes has accidentally dropped some ash on the carpet and burned a mark into it. This person probably didn't stay your friend for much longer after doing that! But as long as the burn is not too deep, then you can cover it up yourself quite simply. First you need to vacuum up any ashes and burnt carpet fibers. Then, take a piece of fine sandpaper and rub it across the burnt tips of the fibers that are still attached to the carpet. Vacuum a second time, and voila! No more burn stain.

No Wax?

Many modern kitchens come furnished with floors described as "no wax." You've probably noticed that these floors are quite easy to clean, so long as you wash them everyday (for a really great sparkle, you might want to add a spoonful of vinegar to the water). But if your kitchen is several days old, and you notice some dulling on the floors that washing won't eliminate, then what can you do? Wax it! No wax floors are essentially treated with a special type of wax that has a limited lifetime. Once that wax wears down, there is no reason not to replace it.

Organization is Key

You've probably gotten the idea by now that the best way to approach cleaning your house is through a structured and organized system or routine. Never vacuum first and then dust, or you will find yourself having to re-vacuum any stray dust. Likewise, always put things in their proper places before you start vacuuming, or else you will have to keep turning the vacuum cleaner on and off as you put things away— turning it on and off in such a way will increase your electrical bill tremendously!

Ceramic Certainties

If you have a wall in your home that is covered with ceramic tiling, then here is a method that is certain to get it clean. Most of the cleansers that you can buy in stores work just fine for such tiling, so there is no need to mix any kind of homemade concoction. The secret is how you use the sponge, not the cleanser! Wipe down a small area of the wall at a time, and keep washing the sponge with clean water. That way you will prevent yourself from recirculating the dirt along the wall.

Candle Troubles

Candles are a beautiful way to illuminate any room, perfect for large parties or intimate and romantic evenings. But candles drip wax quite profusely, and if you

113

are not careful you will find large globs of it on your carpet. If some candle wax spills onto your carpet, then don't try to scrape it off, or you will tear out some carpet fibers. Instead, place a paper bag over the wax spill and turn your iron on. Rub the iron over the bag, and the wax will start to melt. The fibers of the bag will suck up a considerable amount of the wax, and the rest you can scratch off when it is warm and somewhat liquidy.

Hit the Spot

If you think cleaning your walls sounds like a lot of work, then you are right! That's why you should do whatever you can to minimize the work load. Take a good look at the walls in each of your rooms. Do they all really need cleaning? Perhaps only one or two per room are dirty. Is the entire wall dirty, or does only a small portion of it need to be cleaned? If so, just clean the spot. Remember, you clean your house so you can get more enjoyment from it. You won't get any enjoyment from it if you spend all your time cleaning it!

Wicked Webs

My mother always told me never to kill spiders because they ate other insects. That may be true, but I hate it when I encounter spider webs in my home. Not only do they look terrible and messy, but they even give the impression that a home is actually unsanitary. Many people suggest sucking up cobwebs with a vacuum cleaner with a hose attachment, but I have found that it is better to simply use a broom. Make sure the broom is clean and fairly soft, so that you don't leave any messy streaks or scratches on your walls or ceilings. And don't forget to remove the spider before you clean the cobweb!

Cover Up

If you've ever looked really closely at the walls in your kitchen, then you've probably noticed the greasy stains left behind from spilled coffee, oil from pans, and a whole variety of other sources. The key to dealing with such a problem is covering it up with contact paper. Contact paper is much easier to clean than a wall is (it usually wipes clean with a sponge and warm water), and if a stain ever occurs that is so tough that you can't get it out, then simply tear off the contact paper and put a new batch up! You can even buy contact paper that is perfectly translucent, so no one will even know that it is there.

Driveway Drips

Many floors around your house are made out of asphalt, concrete, or stone. Your basement and driveway are two examples of locations with such flooring. The secret to cleaning up a spill in such an area is not to use a mop or brush; cleaning tools like this will simply spread the mess everywhere! Sprinkle kitty litter over the spill; this substance is remarkably absorbent, more so than any sponge I've ever encountered, and in less than a day it will have solidified even the worst spill. Then you can use a broom to clean up this solid mess.

Will it Work?

Here's a handy hint to help you choose the best cleanser to keep your floor spotless. Some cleansers react poorly with different types of surfaces, so it is best to test them in an inconspicuous corner of the room. Put a few small dabs of the cleanser on the floor, wait several minutes, and then rub it off with a rag. If it damages the finish, then don't use it elsewhere! If there is no problem, then you know you can use it.

Try a Template

Here's another suggestion for working with cleansers. Even if you have tested a cleanser on the appropriate surface, as described above, you still don't want to get more of it on the floor than necessary. As such, it's a good idea to make a template for the area you want to clean. Take a piece of cardboard, such as the kind that backs dress shirts, and cut a hole in it about the same size and shape as the stain. Then, when scrubbing the cleanser into the stain, you can be certain that it won't spread too far.

Clean Smelling Carpet

You know that box of baking soda you keep in the back of your refrigerator to absorb foul odors? We all know how well this substance works, so why do we only use it in the fridge? Baking soda is one of the best things you can buy to rid your carpet of all the horrible smells lurking within its fibers. Simply sprinkle it over your carpet and allow it to soak up the smells for an hour or two. Then vacuum it up. You will be amazed how much more lovely the entire room smells!

Hide and Seek

Why do we clean our home? So that it looks neat and tidy. Therefore, as long as an area is not unsanitary, we can consider covering up anything unsightly as a form of cleaning. You've probably noticed in your kitchen that the floor beneath the breakfast table is extremely scuffed from pulling the chairs in and out. You have also probably wanted to do something about this ugly circumstance, but don't want to spend a lot of effort trying to deal with scuff marks. Why not just place a mat or rug under the table and chairs? That way no one can see the blemishes.

Problem Areas

If walls are just flat expanses, then how could they possibly have problem areas? You have to remember that they are not just flat expanses. They have baseboards, electrical outlets, windows, etc. The one thing I can guarantee you about cleaning is that there will always be problem areas! The best tool for dealing with such areas is a toothbrush. Clean the areas just as you would the rest of the wall, but use the toothbrush so you can attend to it very accurately. And whenever you come close to an electrical outlet, be very careful; even a few drops of water in an outlet is enough to give you a very serious shock!

Remember the Outside

Whenever people decide it's time to clean their walls, they generally forget one very important set of walls: the ones outside your home! If you clean these walls once or twice every year, you will probably end up saving yourself thousands of dollars, because you will protect your finish, and this means you won't have to repaint or refinish the exterior as often. There are so many different methods and devices for cleaning your outside walls that I can't even begin to go into them all here. Just consider this a friendly reminder to do it. Your best bet is to go to a hardware store and discuss with a representative the type of finish you have on your home and the budget you have for cleaning it. He or she will be able to tell you whether or not you need to rent any special equipment, what cleansers will not harm your finish, and how to do the job safely.

Rug Rinsing

Many of us have a wonderful rug that was handed down to us from generations past—it almost seems a shame to walk on such a gorgeous heirloom! As such,

117

it is important not to forget to clean them fairly regularly. You should clean them outside in your yard, on top of a plastic tarpaulin or several garbage bags. Wash the rug with a solution of cold water and dishwashing detergent, and then rinse it clean with a hose. Don't spray too hard, or you might damage the rug. In order to dry it, it is best to hang it on a line, but be aware that this method of drying often takes up to 2 full days.

Stop Scuffs

Whenever you clean your walls, floor, or ceiling, you probably find that you have to move some of the furniture around. But some people move it very inefficiently, first to one side of the floor, then to the other. This increases your chances of scuffing the floor a great deal, and a scuff is a very difficult mark to get out! The way to move furniture the least is to work in small sections. In other words, clean one part of the floor at a time. Move the furniture out of that area, clean it, then put the furniture back. Then move on to a new area. Another safety precaution you can use is to put cushy towels under the legs of your furniture. That way, even if you drag the furniture, it won't leave a scuff mark.

Rearranging Remnants

If you've ever been taken by the sudden urge to rearrange your living room or bedroom (and who of us hasn't?), then you probably know how disappointing it is to see the beautiful results of your hard work marred by dents that were created in the carpet by your furniture in its previous location. You've probably run up to the dents and kicked at them, trying to motivate the carpet fibers to spring back to their upright position. The secret to making the dents disappear is so simple you wouldn't believe it! Simply set your iron to the steam function, and hold it about one inch above the dent. Eventually you will notice the fibers starting to stand up again.

Never Ever

Here are a few things you should never ever do when cleaning your carpets. First, don't squeeze any lemon or drop any vinegar onto blood stains. I know I have been talking about lemons and vinegar as if they can clean anything, but these are highly acidic substances, and acid creates a chemical reaction in blood which makes the stain even worse than before. Second, never heat up a stain. Some people think heating it up will make it more manageable and easier to remove the spill, but it usually just embeds it deeper into the carpet fibers. And third, never use any harsh chemicals on carpets, or you will obliterate the dye that colors your carpet.

Real Repairs

As walls have such large, uninterrupted expanses, any defect on them is extremely visible. Go to your walls right now. Do the places that look dirtiest have small cracks in the paint, nicks in the drywall, etc.? You should seriously consider fixing these marks (no, you don't have to redo the entire wall!), as it will make your home look much cleaner. Nicks and scratches have a tendency to catch dirt. I know that this might seem to be a rather extreme measure to take to make your home look clean, but why not go all the way? It really isn't that difficult to patch up a small crack with filler putty and to get the color of your paint matched at a local hardware store.

Windows, Drapes and Doors

Hanging Blinds

To keep hanging blinds (the ones where the slats hang vertically) dust-free and shiny, simply wipe them with a clean, dry rag. But if they get somewhat sticky or tacky for any reason, and the dust sticks to them, then dunk them in sudsy water until clean. You might have to use a little bit of elbow grease.

Horizontal Blinds

Horizontal blinds can be a little bit more tricky then hanging blinds, especially because their slats tend to be narrower. For general or day-to-day dusting, a handheld vacuum will usually do the trick. If they get sticky, however, then you will have to remove the blinds and spray them down with a garden hose. Be careful when using the hose: if you use too much water pressure, the slats will buckle—just use enough to remove the grime.

Sparkling Windows

It's a clear and beautiful day outside . . . or is it? Many people can't answer this question, due to the grime that has accumulated on their windows. You can spend literally hundreds of dollars each year on glass cleaners that allegedly cut down grease and won't leave streaks, but we all know that these products often don't work. The solution to your problem is so simple that you probably have it sitting in your kitchen closet right now: vinegar. Simply add a few spoonfuls of vinegar to a bucket of water, and scrub down your windows. Not only will you be able to see the beautiful world outside, but the added light penetrating your home will make it look cleaner!

Plastic Problems

Due to their tough resistance to shattering, many houses now come equipped with plastic windows. One type of such plastic is called Plexiglas. These substances are entirely different than glass. If you are not careful, then you could scratch them very easily. To clean plastic windows properly, first douse them with water. Then take a clean and soft cloth and dip it in a mixture of water and lemon juice. Gently rub the plastic. Be sure not to wipe the pane dry, as this will almost definitely scratch it. Simply let it air dry. Surprisingly, this will leave no streaks.

Filthy Frames

Everyone knows that you have to keep your windows clean, but it is so easy to forget that the frames should be kept clean too! If you go to your window right now, I am sure you will be shocked at the amount of dirt that has settled on the frame! Toothbrushes are the best tools for cleaning window frames, as their brush areas are about the same size as most standard frames. You usually won't even need any kind of soap or detergent, but if you do, then vinegar or glass cleaner will do the trick just fine. Incidentally, it is best to clean the frame *before* attending to the window.

Shutter Trouble

Due to all of their annoying nooks and crannies, shutters can be a real hassle to keep clean. I think the best way to rid them of dust is simply to vacuum them down with a handheld vacuum. If this doesn't work, then you'll just have to get out your rag and start cleaning one slat at a time. Shutters may look beautiful, but now you understand why they aren't so common anymore!

Dirty Doors

It's not something you think about too often, but you touch the doors in your house literally dozens of times each day. If you go and inspect the area around your door knobs right now, then you will probably find horrible black fingerprints and other marks. Just think about how many times you've touched the door knob while your hands have been very dirty! You should clean door knobs and doors with soap and warm water at least twice a month. If you haven't done this recently, then you will probably need to scrub extra hard, and might even have to use a cleanser.

Doors That Squeak and Creak

There's nothing more aggravating than a closet or hallway door that squeaks, but for some reason you always put off attending to it. Well here's the easiest way to fix it. Go down to a hardware store and ask the manager to help you find silicone lubricant. One or two dabs or sprays of this will take care of that pesky hinge that has annoyed you for so long.

Clear Windows

There's nothing as nice as being able to wake up in the morning and look at the beautiful snowy landscape outside. But if jack frost has been nipping at your window, then you won't have much of a view. Simply open the window, apply some rubbing alcohol to the outside, and wipe it off with loosely crumpled newspaper.

Streakless Wonder

The product you used to clean the window promised it wouldn't leave streaks. Even the vinegar method suggested above claimed it would leave your windows sparkling and new. So what's wrong with your windows? Nothing at all! The problem is the way you clean the windows. Throw out all the old rags you use to wipe them down, because they are the culprits causing the nasty streaks. The best way to clean a window without leaving streaks is to scrub it with a piece of lightly crumpled newspaper! Why? Nobody knows, but it works.

Smoking Smudges

If you live in a household of smokers, then chances are your windows get dirty very often. It is even possible that they get so dirty that you've forgotten how clean they can be! In my experience, the best way to clean smoke stains from a pane of glass is with rubbing alcohol. Smoke, unlike many other types of dirt, actually creates a layer that coats the entire pane, and this layer must be "eaten away." If you mix a solution of equal parts rubbing alcohol and warm water, then you should have no trouble removing this layer. The odor should even disappear with it. Enjoy the clean view!

Beautiful Bamboo

Bamboo shades are a beautiful way to accent your rooms, but vast amounts of dirt can get stuck to their smooth surfaces. They are also extremely delicate, so scrubbing too hard will break them. In order to clean them properly, you should remove them from the wall, lay them on a soft towel on top of a flat table, and rub them gently with a mixture of water and dishwashing detergent.

Tough Dirt

Sometimes a really tough piece of dirt gets stuck on your window pane. The problem with trying to clean this type of dirt is that you have to resist the temptation to use lots of force, or else you might accidentally shatter the glass and seriously injure yourself. The first technique you should try is to scrape it off carefully with a razor blade (don't cut yourself!). This method even works well with residue from glues and paints. If that doesn't work, then take a soft brush and keep rubbing the dirt until it comes off. Use plenty of soap and water, so that you don't scratch the surface of the glass. Once the dirt is gone, give the window a general cleaning with the method described in the entry above.

Got a Light?

The razor blade technique mentioned above will almost always work flawlessly, but every now and then you are bound to run into some kind of dirt that gives it a bit of trouble. Rather than scraping at the dirt repeatedly (and risking cutting yourself), try loosening the grit by dabbing it with lighter fluid. This liquid can cut through almost anything! Then you can easily scrape the dirt away.

Dull Drapes

Imagine standing in front of an open window for just one week. Think about all the dirt that would fly in and hit you on the face, all the rain drops that would smear the dirt and create yucky grime, etc. So why do people wonder how their drapes get so dirty? The best way to keep them clean is by opening the window only when necessary. In order to clean them once they are already dirty, try vacuuming them. This usually does the trick, so vacuum them frequently. If they need a more serious cleaning, then read the label. Some can be machine washed, but others need hand washing or even dry cleaning.

Aluminum's Alright

Many modern houses come furnished with windows that have aluminum frames. They are not only beautiful to look at, but they are practical as well (if you ever remodel your home in the future, I recommend you look into the possibility of replacing your existing windows with aluminum framed ones). The reason these windows are so great is because they slide very easily—they won't stick in the summer, like wooden window frames always do—and because one half usually comes out. This makes it very easy to clean! Just be careful when you remove it, because you could cut yourself badly if you dropped it.

Screen Screams

One of the most difficult portions of your windows to clean are the bug screens. These screens are vital, as they really do prevent all sorts of insects from entering your home, but so much dirt can get clogged in them that they can make you want to scream. The best way to clean them is to remove them from the window. First get rid of all the large pieces of dust using your vacuum cleaner hose. Then, lean it up against a tree or have someone hold it, and spray it down with a hose (just make sure that person doesn't mind getting wet). Use a strong brush to scrape off any really worn in dirt, and keep spraying with the hose until it is clean. Once it has dried, you can return it to the window.

If It Ain't Broke . . .

We've all heard the old saying, "If it ain't broke, don't fix it!" Often, when you're done cleaning, you'll notice a tiny little spot that you've missed, and it will drive you crazy for the rest of the day. I advise that you never try to fix a little spot like this, or you really

125

will make a big mess out of your mostly clean window. In trying to clean the spot, you'll probably leave streaks everywhere else! So remember, just because it has a tiny bit of dirt on it doesn't mean it's broken.

Clothing and Laundry

Laundry. The very word itself is depressing. It's that one chore that you will do anything to put off, even to the point of dusting the living room a second time. You hate it because things always go wrong. Colors bleed. Pants and shirts come out wrinkled. Why can't it ever turn out right for once?

Relax! Laundry doesn't have to be your worst nightmare. There are plenty of little things you can do to make it easier and more successful. Just follow the hints below, and you're bound to have far fewer problems. This will be a great relief to you, and you will feel a wonderful sense of satisfaction as you spend some fun afternoons with your family, knowing that the only reason you have this free time is because you now know how to do the wash more quickly and efficiently!

Caring for Your Clothes
Helpful Labels
Here is the most important hint on how to keep your laundry clean: always read the *label!* I am always surprised to hear how many people ignore the care labels on their apparel. The manufacturer put these labels on so that you would know how to take care of your purchase, so make sure you read them! It will save you a great deal of trouble in the long run.

Simplify by Sorting
Another common mistake is that people really don't know how to sort their clothes correctly before washing them. There are three categories you should sort into: lights, darks, and others. "Others" include anything that might be problematic, such as clothes which

create lint. Naturally, depending on your wash load, you could have many different subcategories of clothes, all of which are "other." People always wonder whether certain colors, such as light blue, should be considered lights or darks. The best I advice I can give is that you should use your own judgment. If a light blue shirt is brand new, then wash it in cold with your darks, as it might bleed in warm water. Once it is a few months old, you can wash it in warm with your lights.

Expensive Ironing

Irons suck up a huge amount of electricity, so it is always best not to iron a garment if you think it looks acceptable the way it is. If you do have to iron certain pieces of clothing, wait until you have several to do. That way, you won't waste electricity by waiting for it to get hot many times. Another neat little trick to remember is to turn off the iron before you're finished with it. There is usually enough heat left for you to iron at least one or two last garments before you put it away.

Sheer Clothes

We've all discovered those annoying little balls of fluff that appear on certain pieces of clothing after they have been removed from the laundry. Aren't they terrible? The solution to this problem is extremely simple. Get out the old electric shaver that is sitting in your medicine chest, and "sheer" the balls off your clothing. You do have to be careful when doing this, or you might create a snag, but you'll find that this works like a charm.

Lint Busters

Lint is one of the easiest problems to solve when it comes to doing your laundry. Simply turn items inside out that tend to create lint. Such items include sweaters, towels, and certain socks. Another handy thing to remember is that these items should be washed separately from the rest of the laundry.

Cheeky Chocolate

Almost everyone loves chocolate, and if you're anything like me, sometimes it seems hard to go through a whole day without some, but apart from being very bad for your figure, it is also quite a difficult stain to remove. Try to get to the stain before it dries out, and scratch off as much of the residue as possible with your fingernail. Use gentle motions, or you can make the stain even harder to remove. Then dab the spot with a special chemical called dry spotter, which is similar to the chemical used by dry cleaners (as with any chemicals, always read the directions in order to use it effectively and safely). Finally, wash the garment in cold water, and you will find that the stain is usually gone. If, however, some of it remains, do not dry it, or this will make it permanent! Wash it over and over again until you can no longer see the spot.

Terrific Ties

Many people wonder how you should clean a tie. The answer is simple: you shouldn't! Ties are extremely delicate, and they will be destroyed if you try to clean them too often. If a stain does get on your tie, then take it in to be dry-cleaned. There are some methods for cleaning ties at home with water, but they seriously jeopardize the article of clothing. So try not to spill soup on your tie next time!

Sudsy Soaking

Whenever you have any clothes that are severely stained, you should soak them first. The best way to soak your clothes is to fill the washer with water (either warm or cold, depending on whether you are washing lights or darks). Put in your stained garments, and then add the proper amount of detergent, as indicated on the instructions to the detergent. Let the garments sit in this soapy water for at least two hours.

Irksome Ink

We all know that horrible feeling of realizing that a ball-point pen has just exploded in our pocket, drenching our favorite shirt or pair of pants in blue ink. The first thing you should do is cry! You have to be honest with yourself that the chances of fixing this garment are amazingly slim, as pen ink is virtually impossible to remove. If you want to try getting it out, then here is the best method. Hold the stain under a faucet and turn on the warm water; grasp the garment in such a way that the water can run through it without coming into contact with any other area of the clothing, or you might inadvertently transfer part of the stain. When it seems like no more of the stain will rinse out, douse the spot with hair spray and tap it dry with a rag. Some more of the ink should come off. Then wash the garment in warm water as you would regularly, and cross your fingers that everything will turn out okay!

Permanent Problems

If you have children, then you probably have some permanent markers lying around the house. As with the entry about ball-point pens above, permanent marker stains are almost more trouble trying to remove than they are worth, but you can occasionally have some success getting rid of them. Douse the offending spot with hair spray, allow this to soak in, and then rinse it clean with warm water. You should notice some improvement. Then toss the garment into the machine and clean it as you normally would. If you get to the stain quickly enough, then you might be pleasantly surprised with your results.

Inefficient Overload

Many people erroneously think that overloading the washer and dryer will save them money on their energy bills in the long run. This couldn't be further from the truth! In the first place, overloading these appliances makes them work harder. In the second place, they don't work as well; clothes might come out of the washer so dirty that you have to rewash them, and they will certainly not be dry. And in the third place, everything will be so crumpled that you will *have to* get out the iron if you want your clothes to look presentable. If your clothes still come out wrinkled, then try putting a damp towel in with your clothes once they are already dry. Turn the dryer on for a few more minutes, and voila!

Baby Blots

Baby food, as nutritious as it may be, stains more quickly and easily than just about any other food you can buy. The most effective approach to cleaning it is by preventing stains from occurring in the first place; in other words, purchase the largest bib you can find for your baby! Remove as much of the stain as you can by scraping it or running it under water. You should be aware that baby's food has a high concentration of sugar in it, so when you apply a detergent, make sure it is not highly acidic (something the label will tell you), or this will make the stain even worse. Also, when cleaning off a sugar, only use cold water—if you want to know why, then just consider the fact that cotton candy is simply heated up sugar!

Iron Phobia

Many people have a horrible phobia about turning on an iron because they are certain that anything they touch will immediately burn to a crisp. If you are one of these poor people, then here are a few guidelines to help you on the road to recovery from iron phobia. First, always rest the iron in such a way that its hot plate is not coming into contact with anything (including your delicate skin!) when you are not moving it constantly; in other words, never leave it in one spot on a garment for more than a few seconds. Second, spray some water onto items of clothing that are very wrinkled. You will probably have to put some elbow grease into dealing with them, so the added water will help prevent any burns. Third, any highly textured item should be ironed inside out. This is also usually the case for somewhat delicate items that can be ironed (please read the label carefully when attempting to iron these items). And fourth, always unplug the iron when you are not using it. It is frighteningly easy to start a fire with an iron!

Clean Showers

Not many people are aware of this, but many shower curtains can be cleaned in the washing machine, as long as you take it out prior to the spin cycle. That grime on shower curtains is almost impossible to clean in any other way, but this usually does the trick. As most shower curtains are at least partially made of plastic, you shouldn't put them in the dryer. Hang them on a line to dry, straightening them as much as possible in order to avoid wrinkles.

Napkin Prevention

Many of the other chapters you have already read in this book have entries dealing with preventing messes from occurring in the first place. Well, this chapter is no different, so here are a few tips to help prevent you from staining your clothes, and as such from needing to remove those stains. First, whenever you eat, put a napkin on your lap. Until a few years ago, this very sensible suggestion was a part of common courtesy, but now that seems to have disappeared forever (much to the dismay of mothers everywhere!). Second, whenever you eat very messy food, such as a hamburger, place a napkin around the food to catch any dribbles.

Appropriate Attire

You just stained your favorite silk blouse? You got a dab of paint on a good blazer? How are you ever going to get these stains out? The answer is simple: you aren't! It absolutely amazes me that people wear their best clothes into the worst situations. If you know you are going somewhere where you are likely to sully your clothes, such as a greasy spoon, then why wear good clothes? Take an old pair of jeans that you won't mind staining. That way, if the spot doesn't come out, you won't mind!

Creative Cutting

Here is another creative approach to getting rid of stains you don't like on slightly shabbier clothes (such as slacks or flannel shirts): cut the stain off entirely. I'm not talking about cutting a hole in the garment, but rather turning it into a pair of shorts or a short sleeved shirt. Obviously, if the spot is in a place where such cutting is not possible, you cannot do this, but there are plenty of other creative options open to you. You could, for example, sew a patch over it, or even hide it with a brooch!

Buy More Than One Hamper

Why do most households have just one laundry hamper? Wouldn't it be better to have several, so that everyone could just toss their dirty clothes into the appropriate ones? They could put colors in one, whites in another, etc. If your family is conscientious about this, then you can significantly reduce the amount of time it takes you to do laundry, as you won't have to sort clothes anymore.

Soap Situation

A lot of people put their clothes in the washer and then pour soap on top. Unless your machine has an agitator (the little dish on top which slowly releases the detergent), this can defeat the whole purpose of doing your laundry. The soap will tend to stay at the top, so only the uppermost clothes in the machine will be properly washed. Instead, you should put the soap in first and add clothes as the washer starts to fill up with sudsy water.

Simply Delicate

Here's a great and inexpensive way to wash your delicate articles of clothing in your washing machine. Simply arrange them inside a pillowcase and tie it shut! There's no hassle to this method whatsoever.

Oily Solutions

Two of the oiliest places on most people's bodies are their neck and wrists. You've probably noticed that your clothes seem to wear out in these spots before anywhere else. To help preserve your clothes and save you the agony of trying to remove stains, encourage your family to wipe these areas with rubbing alcohol prior to dressing.

Iron Now, Not Later

A good way to save time when doing your laundry is to iron immediately after you remove clothes from the dryer. This way, you don't have to separate the clothes twice (once after drying, and then again after ironing). You can also save even more time, because the best time to iron clothes is when they are slightly damp. Turn your dryer off 5 minutes before the timer would normally do, and iron. The ironing itself will complete the drying, and your clothes will be even more wrinkle-free!

Press, Don't Pull

Most people don't realize it, but there are several ways to iron. Any time you are ironing a delicate fabric, or are trying to create a pleat or sharp fold, you should press the garment. This means that rather than pushing and pulling the iron along it, you should press down with the iron in one spot, lift it, and then press down on another spot. Turn clothes inside out when pressing, and use a press cloth when working with delicates.

Aluminum Ironing Board

A great way to speed up ironing is to wrap your ironing board in aluminum foil. Never iron directly onto the aluminum foil, however, as this could be dangerous; always cover the foil with an ironing pad. The foil catches the heat and projects it back upwards, so you virtually iron both sides at once! Most people don't know this, but the two sides of foil are different. Wrap the board in such a way that the shinier side is facing up.

Button Down Solution

Tired of having to struggle to remove clothes from the washer because the sleeves of shirts have gotten wrapped around all the other clothing? Why not simply button the cuffs to the front of the shirt? This idea will save you plenty of time each time you wash a load.

Proper Air

All fabrics are porous materials; as such, like our skin, they need to breathe. Leather is especially sensitive to this, but other fabrics also require fresh air. You should never cover your clothes completely. Remove them from the plastic bags in which dry cleaners put them as soon as you get home. To prevent them from getting dirty, you might want to wrap them in a loose material that is also porous. For example, you can hang a sheet in your closet to cover your entire wardrobe.

Really White

When washing a load of whites, bleach works best if added after the load has been in the machine for a few minutes on the wash cycle. Also, don't be afraid to use really hot water. The key to using temperature successfully is to be careful when separating your clothing; if you know you're going to wash your whites on hot, then don't put any colors in that load.

Where to Put Clothes

This may sound silly, but always put your most recently washed clothing at the back of the closet or on the bottom of the pile of folded clothes. That way, you won't wear these clothes again right away, and they will last longer.

Use and Care of Appliances

Washing the Washer

Detergents can be harsh on the inside of your washing machine, and after a few months, excessive amounts of residue can build up. To clean out the washer, simply set it on hot and run it empty for an entire cycle. Instead of adding detergent to the water, however, add vinegar. Use the vinegar sparingly and only every now and then, as the acidity could eventually damage the machine.

Clean the Lint Screen

Cleaning the lint screen is the most important regular maintenance you can perform on your dryer. As well as enabling clothes to dry more quickly, thereby saving you money on your utility bills, it can prevent the dryer from getting too hot and catching fire! Simply wiping the lint off each time you use it is not enough. Every week or two you should scrub it with soap and warm water; make sure to rinse well, so no soap builds up on it. Be sure that it is fully dry before replacing it in the machine.

Iron Solid

When you hear the word appliance, then you probably only think of your washer and dryer. But don't forget that your iron is an appliance too, and that you need to take care of it in order to keep it running. When using the mist function on your iron, it is very important that the water is clean! The best water to use is distilled water from bottles, which will leave no deposits whatsoever. Pour out any excess water while the iron is still hot.

Smoothing Scratches

If you are not very careful with your iron, then it is easy to scratch the heating plate. This can be terrible for clothes, creating snags and even tears in fabric, and must be attended to immediately. The solution is to sand down the plate with extra fine grade sandpaper. Your iron won't look so pretty anymore, but it will work just fine. Some scratches may be so deep that the only thing you can do is throw it out.

Icky Irons

As you now know, irons are not only useful when doing the laundry, but they can even help you out when working on your carpet! So why not keep your iron clean and running well? It is hardly surprising that the hot plate itself gets quite dirty, considering it has to be rubbed across a great many articles of clothing. Clean this with a moist rag, and never use any kind of detergents or scouring agents. The steam chamber should be cleaned after each use. Empty it out and fill it with pure mineral water. Heat this water up and then allow it to steam for a few seconds. Finally, make sure to shake out all of the mineral water when you are done.

Quick Tips

Keep an empty coffee can or some other type of container handy to place all coins, papers, and anything else that inevitably turns up in pants pockets.

Save all instructions, tags and labels from various clothing and pin them up on a bulletin board for easy reference.

Keep a cloth or plastic "charity" bag in an out-of-the-way spot to hold worn, outgrown, or outdated clothes that can be given away to those in need.

Build a shelf or two to hold all of your laundry supplies—detergent, bleach, softener, etc.—in one central location.

Keep a pair of scissors handy for snipping off loose threads.

Wash socks together in a bag sewn from a net-like material. This way, you will never end up with an odd sock after washing and drying!

Wipe down the washer, dryer, hot water heater, shelves and anything else in the room to keep them dust free.

Keep hangers in the laundry room so that you can easily and immediately hang up your clothing when emptying the dryer. Place the hangers on hooks attached to the walls.

Stand or hang your ironing board up against a wall to keep it out of the way.

Keep the tops of your washer and dryer free of clutter.

If you have the room, build a countertop on which

you can sort your dirty laundry and fold your clean clothes. If space is scarce, then at least use laundry baskets for sorting dirty laundry. The idea here is to keep all of your clothing off of the floor.

Garage and Yard

If you're like most people, then your garage has become a place where you almost fear to go. So many year's worth of odds and ends that don't really belong in any other room have piled up so high that you can barely walk through the garage, let alone park your car inside of it at night. Well, this is the chapter you've been waiting for. You'll learn to tame the savage beast that your once clean garage has become!

Next, you'll discover how to take care of your possessions outside of your house, including some basic hints about keeping your lawn beautiful. If you happen to have a pool, then you'll probably benefit from the advice you'll read here. And there's also a few words about your home's exterior.

Organizing Your Garage
Hold a Garage or Yard Sale
Let's face it, you don't need or want half the things in your garage, so why not participate in an American tradition and hold a garage or yard sale? If you don't try to make too much of a profit, then you'll probably be able to sell well over half of the junk that is littering your floor. You'll be on the road to a more organized garage in no time!

Use the Walls
The key to organizing a garage is getting everything off the floor. Almost anything that you keep in your garage can be suspended on the wall. All power tools should be kept on a peg board screwed into the wall. All sports equipment, such as bicycles or kids' soccer nets, should be fastened to the wall with special hooks,

or even hung from the rafters with durable cord (if the rafters are tall enough—you don't want to scrape the roof of your car by mistake). Put the things that you use most often close to the ground, and those that are used less frequently higher up.

Future Sales

If your first garage sale was a success, you'll probably have more in the future. But don't allow your garage to accumulate junk like it did before. Instead, whenever you think that you might not want an item anymore, put it in a special box marked "Garage Sale." Once you have accumulated four or five boxes, have another sale.

Shoe Bags

As in other areas of your home, shoe bags are great ways to organize the garage. Hang several of them up in different areas, so that different types of items don't get mixed up. For example, hang one near your work bench to organize tools and gloves. Hang another near your lawn mower to organize gardening supplies such as work boots and small spades.

Parking Spaces

A garage is a room shared by everyone in the family, so why not assign everyone his or her own space? Mom's car should be parked on the left, Dad's car on the right, Junior's bicycle in this corner, the snow tractor in that corner. You should even spray paint the lines for the different "parking spaces," so that no one accidentally intrudes on anyone else's area. Furthermore, divide your garage into areas designated for specific activities, for instance tools, sporting equipment, gardening supplies, barbecuing equipment,

145

automobile supplies, etc. Assign the most convenient spots in your garage to those activities which you practice the most often. This idea is especially good for people who have trouble remembering plans. Just as creating a small chart for the closet in your bedroom helps you remember where everything goes, so will painting these lines remind you of how to organize your garage.

Garbage Cans

Almost everyone has more garbage cans than they need, so why waste valuable space? Take any that you are not using and clean them thoroughly with soap and a hose. Once they have dried, line them with a strong garbage bag or a cloth sack and store various items in them. They're especially good for things like hoses and electrical cords which can be difficult to wind up neatly.

Inventory

No matter how organized you are, you are always going to have a few boxes filled with stuff in the garage. But even this can be ordered. Make sure that similar items are found in the same box. Then make an inventory list of the contents and staple it to the side of the box that is in plain view.

No More Oil

Even a well organized garage seems to be plagued by the problem of oil that has dripped from your car onto the ground. The magic ingredient to make such stains disappear is cat box litter. Pour the litter very liberally over the stain, and allow it to sit for a few hours. Then scrub it in with all your might, using a brick or some other heavy and coarse object. Finally, brush away the litter, and *voila!* Don't forget to get your car looked at, because the leak might be serious.

Open and Shut Case

Cracked paint on garage doors is not only unsightly, but it can also cause considerable damage as well. Paint prevents humidity from swelling the wood in the summertime. If your door swells too much, then it could get stuck, and you could break it very easily while trying to open it. Painting a garage door shouldn't take more than a single day, and it is well worth the investment to increase the beauty and durability of the home in which you live.

Now That You Can Park Your Car . . .

Once your garage is well ordered enough for you to be able to bring your car back in, you can make the difficult task of parking a little easier with the following idea. Attach a tennis ball to the end of a long piece of cord. Hang the cord from the ceiling of your garage, about a foot from the back wall. Adjust the length of the cord so that the tennis ball is just below the height of the hood of your car. That way, whenever you park, you know you are far enough in when you nudge against the ball.

Check Your Lights

Install mirrors in your garage so that you can check both your car's headlights and taillights before leaving. Place one mirror in an inside front corner, the other in an inside back corner, positioning each at a slight angle. Check the placement when you're in the driver's seat—you should be able to see the headlights in the front mirror and the taillights in the back mirror when looking in your rear-view mirror.

147

Soft Landings

If you like to use your power tools in the workshop in your garage, then you've probably felt your heart sink as you accidentally drop one of them into the hard cement ground below. You think to yourself of all the money you've wasted because of your absentmindedness. The solution to this problem is so simple that you've probably never even thought of it before: put a layer of foam padding on the floor!

Winterize Your Tools

If you live in a cold climate, it's a good idea to winterize your garden tools. First, clean off any dirt. Then coat the wood parts lightly with linseed oil and the metal parts lightly with floor wax. This will prevent the wood from drying and keep the metal from corroding.

Lawnmower Hibernation

Store your lawnmower for the winter using the same rationale. First, empty out all gasoline; just to make sure, run the engine until it dies to burn the last few drops. Take out the spark plugs, and oil the cylinders. Pull the starter to spread the oil around the cylinders. Then put the spark plug back and empty the crankcase of oil.

Working in Your Yard

Slippery Snow Shovel

One of the worst parts about digging the snow out of your driveway is that it keeps sticking to your shovel. Often, you spend just as much time trying to loosen it from your shovel as you do removing it from the driveway. An easy way to solve this problem is to coat your shovel with a silicone lubricant at the beginning of each season. The snow will literally slide off.

Taped Handles

Gardening tools and winter shovels can get lost outside very easily if you're not careful. You can waste hours trying to find them in your yard. To save yourself a lot of time, wrap the handles in coarse, brightly colored tape. This tape will not only make the tool stand out against a green lawn or white snow, but it will also make the handles "grippier."

Hot and Cold Trees

Did you ever think that the way you landscape your yard could possibly affect your utility bills? It may sound silly, but by properly arranging trees, you can make a drastic difference. Plant deciduous trees near your windows; their leaves will keep your interiors shady during summer, but plenty of light will strike your windows when their leaves haven fallen in the winter. Use perennial trees, such as pine trees, as wind screens. Plant them in such a way as to "catch" the wind before it strikes your house!

Delightful Herbs

If your garlic is too old for you to eat, then here's a way to get the most out of it. Just put the old garlic in a pot in a sunny area, and water it regularly, and voila! Garlic is very easy to grow. And your whole family will appreciate the fresh flavor.

All Tied Up

Climbing vines are one of the most beautiful plants with which to adorn your yard, and they are perfect for increasing your privacy. But sometimes, especially when they're young, it can be very difficult for you to keep them tied to their stakes. One of the best ways of doing this is using the green twist ties that come with garbage bags. Since they're green, they virtually disappear in the vine's leaves.

Gleaming Gardens

Your yard is generally the first impression visitors have of your home, so why not put as much care into maintaining it as you do into the rest of your home? You should treat your garden like a room in your house. That is, it needs to be well organized, with everything put where it belongs, and you will need to attend to it every so often in order to make sure that everything is tidy. There should not be any garden hoses, children's toys, etc. lying around. Not only are these eyesores, but they also increase the chances of someone falling and hurting themselves. Make sure the lawn is cut short and that there are no expansive areas that need to be reseeded, and that the hedges and bushes are neatly trimmed. If you attend to these little chores on a regular basis, then you should have no problem keeping your yard looking beautiful.

Circle Your Tree

If you have a tree in your yard, you can make sure it gets as much rainwater as possible in the fall and winter by clearing a grass-free circle around it. Just take a shovel and dig up the earth around it to loosen the earth. To do it perfectly, loop one end of a rope around the tree trunk and the other around the end of your shovel; that way, when you pull the rope tight you'll know you're at the outside edge of your circle.

Sawdust as Mulch

If you've been doing some sawing recently and now have a pile of sawdust, don't just throw it out. Sprinkle it on your flowers and plants—it makes a good mulch, and helps nourish the soil.

Lubricated Locks

Lubricate your locks about every six months. An easy way to do this is with the graphite of an ordinary pencil (#1 or #2). Just rub the point on both sides of the lock's key, thoroughly covering it. Now slip the key in the lock two or three times. This will enable the graphite to lubricate the lock from the inside.

No Rust Furniture

If you leave patio furniture outside during the rainy season, keep the chairs from rusting by drilling holes into the seats. This way, the rainwater just falls right through, instead of collecting in pools in the seats and causing rust. The holes won't change the chair's comfort, and you can use colorless nail polish to seal the edges of the newly-drilled holes so they won't rust.

Glow-in-the-Dark Clothesline

Believe it or not, sometimes accidents occur when people run into their clothesline at night, because they can't see it. You can make your backyard clothesline visible at night by dabbing some glow-in-the-dark paint on a sponge, then running it along the length of the clothesline. Eerie, isn't it?

Dry Firewood

How can you keep your firewood dry outside if you don't have a shed? Make your own shield. Buy a sheet of corrugated plastic—2 feet by 12 feet is should cover most wood piles—and use it as a cover. Even better, drive two wooden poles into the ground on each side of the pile, then cut appropriate holes into the plastic so that the sheet slides down the poles. Remove logs from underneath on one side, so that the other side of the pile remains higher. That way, rain can slope down the plastic and run off.

Caring for Swimming Pools
Help Out Your Yard
If you only want a shallow pool, such as a pool in which you can swim laps, then here's an interesting way to help out the rest of your yard. By painting the bottom of the pool a dark color like green, instead of the usual light blue, sunlight will reflect off the top of the water. This will help all of the plants in your yard to grow!

Splash in the Spa
Going for a dip in your hot tub or spa is a wonderful way to relax at the end of a long and stressful day. But, like anything else in your home, if you want to be able to enjoy your spa for many years to come without any serious problems, then it has to be cleaned regularly. First of all, you should follow the maintenance schedule as outlined in your owner's manual; different types of pumps and filters need to be cleaned at different intervals. You should also clean the spa or hot tub at least once a month, but always use a very mild cleanser and a soft cloth. Don't use scouring powders, steel wool, or acidic detergents. And always make sure you are clean before you enter the water; did you remember to take a shower first.

Two Toys in One

Put your little one's wading pool inside the sand box you have already built. By smoothing the sand down, you're assuring the pool a snug and safe place to rest, much as professionals do when they build real pools. Moreover, you won't be damaging or taking up an extra portion of your yard. Never leave your child unattended while in a pool!

Heavy Duty

Those wading pools may be small, but they're sure heavy once you've filled them with water! They also seem to get dirty so quickly. To prevent this and save yourself the hassle of having to empty out the water every few days, just keep a bucket of clean water next to the pool. Make your kids clean their feet, hands, and any other dirty places before getting in. This trick works for adult pools too (there's no reason why grown ups shouldn't have to follow the same rules as kids!).

Pool Shed

There's nothing more annoying than seeing your beautiful carpet get muddied by people running in from the pool. An easy way to solve this problem is by erecting an inexpensive metal shack, or even a tent, as a pool shed. Swimmers can dry off and change in it. If you're really handy, then you might want to create a nice shower to wash off the chlorine by hanging a garden hose from a tall rod.

No More Ear Aches

Here's a great little tip that won't help you care for your pool, but it certainly will help you enjoy it even more. If you're prone to those ear aches that so many

153

people get when swimming in chlorinated pools, then dab your ears with a bit of baby oil a few moments prior to jumping in. This oil will lubricate your ears so well that almost no water will get stuck inside!

Caring for the Exterior of Your Home

Painting Your House

You might think that the best way to beautify your home is by painting it, but you're wrong. In fact, if you paint your house more than once every four or five years, you could be doing serious damage. If you paint this frequently, then the layer of paint gets too thick and becomes brittle; as such, it can crack more easily, allowing the elements to get at the bare wood underneath. The best way to keep your paint looking beautiful for years is to paint less frequently, but apply three coats instead of the usual two. When the paint starts to look a little dirty, scrub it with warm water and an industrial soap that won't damage paint. This is also the perfect way to keep vinyl siding looking new.

Proper Painting

Anyone who has ever painted their house before knows the sight of a paint can with paint that has dripped all down its side. This creates a huge mess in the garage, which is where everyone in the entire world seems to store their half-used cans of paint. This is caused by blotting the paint brush against the rim of the can. To prevent this from happening, simply drill a few holes in the "lip" of the rim which fills up with paint and overflows; any time you blot your brush, the paint will drip back into the can. Since your paint will be permanently exposed to air, you must cover the top of the can very tightly with aluminum foil to prevent it from drying out.

Ladder Security

The ladder is one of the most important tools you will use while working on the outside of your home; painting the second story of your house is a good example of this. While you should never use a ladder without someone spotting you, here is a tip to make your ladder more stable, in case your spotter gets momentarily distracted. Using strong shears, cut out two pieces, about six inches long each, from that old tire in your garage that you've been meaning to throw out for so long. Take these two strips and nail them to the bottom of each leg of the ladder. This will increase friction, thereby decreasing the chances of the ladder sliding out from under you.

A Clean Driveway is a Happy Driveway

Keep your driveway clean and attractive by cleaning it regularly. First, hose it down so it's thorougly wet. Then coat it with a thin layer of environmentally-friendly detergent. Brush it into the surface with an old broom, then rinse it off until the water washes it all off.

Oil-Free Driveway

To prevent your driveway from being stained by oil, you can make your own concrete sealant. Boil some linseed oil, then mix it in equal parts with kerosene. Brush one layer thoroughly onto the driveway and/ or garage floor (after you've cleaned it, of course), and let it dry for an hour. Then wipe off any wet spots with a cloth. If oil has already stained your driveway, try mixing three tablespoons of lye with a gallon of water. Then brush it into the stain and let it sit for about half an hour, then brush more in again. Rinse it all off with cold water. *Wear gloves while attempting these methods—you don't want poisonous lye residue or other chemicals on your hands.*

Household Repair and Maintenance

For want of a nail, the battle was lost. So goes an old expression, and it's message should not go unheeded. Keeping your home well-maintained is a necessity—for both financial and safety reasons. In the Introduction to this book, you learned what basic tools you should either own or to which you should have access. In this chapter, I will show you simple hints and tips that will go a long way towards helping you keep your home in tip-top condition. *Caution! When performing any of the following repairs, be certain that you take appropriate safety measures! And never be afraid to call in a professional repairman if you run into serious problems or simply get in over your head.*

General Handiwork Tips

Dust Collector

When drilling into a ceiling or other vertical space, find an old lid of a plastic food container and drill into that first, then slide it down to the base of the drill bit. When you begin drilling for real, you now have a dust collector, and your eyes can focus on the job at hand without having to worry about getting sprayed.

Sticky Screwdriver

When working on an overhead job, prevent your screws, nuts and washers from falling by first lightly coating them with rubber cement so that they stick to your screwdriver. Later, you can wash off the cement easily.

Loose Screws

Corrugated cardboard makes an excellent storage device for loose screws. Next time you disassemble an item, have a freshly-cut side of cardboard handy in which to place the loose screws. It works just like a cartridge belt. Or, if you prefer, keep the loose screws from falling by laying them down on cardboard, then taping them down. Make sure to press down with the tape, on both sides of the screws, so they're snug.

Got a Match?

If a hole is too wide for a screw, coat a few matchsticks or toothpicks with glue and fill up the hole, so that the screw can then bite into them.

Blunt the Nail

Thin pieces of wood split easily when nailed, so if you're about to hammer a nail into a thin piece of wood, blunt the nail first by tapping it a few times directly on the tip. This will allow the nail to push through the wood, which prevents it from splitting.

Backwards Nail

If you're trying to nail into a tight, hard-to-reach spot, don't use two hands awkwardly. Just position your nail "backwards," wedging it into the claws of the hammer with the head of the nail against the back of the hammer and the tip out. Then pound. This way, the back of the head of the hammer helps the process. Once the nail is in a little ways, turn the hammer around and continue normally.

Clean Cut

If you secretly wish for a cleaner, splinter-free cut when sawing through wood, try this. Lay a strip of masking tape across your cut line before you saw. Then saw through the tape as you saw through the wood. The tape prevents splintering, so that when you finish, you have a perfectly clean cut. How about that!

159

Tough Nuts

Anyone who has ever tried to blindly place a washer and nut onto a bolt knows frustration. Prevent this by first bonding the washer to the nut with rubber cement, then proceed. Attempting to hold onto a nut in a tight spot is also tricky, so make it easier by first making a "ring" out of duct tape, so that the sticky side is facing out. That way the nut sticks to you, and you can then put it anywhere you want.

No More Lumps!

Avoid excess glue lumps! Before gluing two pieces together, run plastic tape around the sides of the pieces to be joined. Dab on the glue, stick them together, and let dry. Later, peel off the tape, and voila, no glue lumps. To be extra sure, run a knife around the joint to strip off any straggling glue spots.

Guitar Picks

Guitar picks are little wonders of the handyperson's world. For instance, if you need to apply a small amount of putty to a nick in wood furniture, it's easier to use a guitar pick, because most putty knives are too large and unwieldy. The pick, however, is small and flexible. This means you can apply less putty, and thus have less to clean and sand.

Easy Fold

Sandpaper is not easy to fold, because it's brittle. So if you need to fold it, first run the smooth side across the edge of a table a few times. This creates little creases in the backside, which then allows it to fold easier.

Denim's Last Stand

Don't throw out those old jeans! Denim is very useful for wood-polishing jobs. Cut up your old jeans (avoiding the seams) into scraps of different sizes. You can use a scrap for the last round of polishing varnished or lacquered wood.

Rust-Be-Gone

Carbonated soda (yes, we're talking cola here) actually makes an excellent rust-stripper. If you have a rusted nut or nail, just drop it into a glass of cola and check it in a few hours. Your rust will be gone.

There's a Hole in the Bucket

If your old plastic bucket develops a crack, you don't have to throw it out. It can be easily repaired by melting the plastic together. Just light a candle, hold it up to a knife blade closely, then hold the heated blade against the crack in the bucket, rubbing it gently back and forth. This will cause just enough melting to mold the crack.

Plumbing and Electrical

Leaky Faucets

The most common problem in most households is that annoying drip, drip, drip. But do not fear—it's incredibly easy to repair. Just follow these simple instructions: Turn off the water from under the sink (there will be two knobs on the pipes). Now turn on the faucet and let the remaining water drip out. Remove the faucet handle. You will see either a screw or a nut, so just follow your instincts and unscrew. You can use a drop of oil if it's sticky. Once the handle is removed, remember to save any pieces that come with it, because you will need them later. Unscrew the next nut you see. Remove the assembly, by unscrewing it. At this point, you will see the faulty washer, which is causing your leak problem. Unscrew the screw that holds the washer. Replace the washer. If you have no immediate replacement for it, you'll have to run down to the hardware store. Take the faulty washer with you as a model of size and type to ask for, then buy several so that you can have more on hand for the same job at a later date. (They're cheap, don't worry about it.) Replace everything by following the above instructions in reverse order.

Hot Water

The most effective—and safest on your pipes—method of cleaning a clogged drain is to use very hot water. Every month or so, boil as much water as you can, then dump into each drain—the bathtub and every sink. This will keep any potential clogs from forming, and keep your pipes free of chemical-based products, which are known to damage pipes.

Natural Cleanser

If hot water doesn't clean out your drain, there is still a safer solution than chemicals. First, bail out the still water (preferably into a nearby drain that works). Then, pour one cup of baking soda down the drain, followed immediately by one cup of vinegar. Quickly seal the drain with a plug or dishrag. Leave it for about twenty minutes. The natural chemical reaction of the soda and the vinegar will disintegrate any clogs. When you return, run hot tap water for a few minutes to clear away any remaining detritus.

No Snake?

If you find you need a plumbing snake and do not have one, just use a strong wire, such as a coat hanger. Straighten it out and bend it at the end, then push it into the drain as far as it will go to loosen any clogging.

162

Toothpick Solution

If you find that you have a small leak in a pipe, you can repair it easily by breaking a toothpick and stuffing it into the small hole, then wrapping plumbing tape (thoroughly) over it.

Rubber Hose

For more significant leaks, you'll need some rubber hosing. An automobile hose will do just fine. Split it down the middle with a knife. Now wrap it around the leak, with the leak in the exact center. Secure it in place with a C-clamp (available at hardware stores), or if temporary, a small wrench will do, until the leak stops.

Howling Pipes

If your pipes howl or screech, it's because the straps holding them in are larger than the pipes themselves. The gap causes vibration. To stop the vibration, seal the gap. First, remove the strap. Then, cut off a small section of garden hose and wrap it around the end of the pipe, then reinstall the strap over it. Now it should be tight, and thus, will not vibrate and cause annoying noises.

Banging Pipes

If your pipes "bang," it's due to an air pocket. Your plumbing system has air chambers which are supposed to prevent this, but every now and then air pockets will still form. Most of the time, the air chamber has become waterlogged, so it will need to be drained. Just shut off the water at its source, then open the faucets at their highest and lowest points. Let any water in the pipes run out until all dripping has stopped. Then close the faucets and turn the water back on at the source. Now that the system has been drained, the

163

air chamber is again clear, and you should not have any annoying banging.

Running Toilet

Lift the top of the back of the toilet and check the float ball. Sometimes it collects water, and thus gets weighed down and so cannot pop back up. Unscrew it, shake it and listen for water. If it's okay, screw it back on. Then bend the float arm down a little, so that the water in the tank never rises above about a half-inch over the overflow tube. If it still runs, shut off the valve and replace the whole contraption with a new one.

Running Toilet II

Quite often, the chain that connects the valve to the float arm gets stuck under the valve, preventing it from closing properly. If this continues to occur, remove the chain from the valve, then cut a common plastic straw in half and slip the chain through it. Then replace the chain. The straw should keep the chain in place.

Clogged Head

If you notice that your shower water does not come out in a steady stream, your shower head is probably clogged. To clean it, first remove the head. You'll need two wrenches, one to hold the shower arm steady and the other to unscrew the head from it. But make sure and wrap tape around the head and arm where you're gripping them, so as not to damage anything. Once it's off, rinse the head with water. This will clear away much of the sediment, but not all of it. The next step is to let it sit in a mixture of half-vinegar (a natural cleanser) and half water, to remove lime deposits. After that, scrub it with a bottle brush to make sure, then poke a needle into any last straggler holes to clear them out. Replace it as before, using two wrenches and tape.

Twist and Wrap

When you need to join two wires together, but you don't have a soldering iron, it can still be done safely. Just strip the insulation off the ends of the wire pairs, twist each to its mate and wrap electrical tape around each new union. If possible, stagger the new connections so that they are two inches apart—this will insure that the wires never touch.

Label Your Circuits

Identify the circuits on your circuit breaker, if this is not already done. Once you confirm which circuit is which, label each accordingly on the box, so that you never have to question it again. If you ever need to shut off specific circuits in an emergency, you'll appreciate your foresight. Plus, anyone else who may need to do so will know instantly.

Loud Radio

Here's a handy tip for working on electrical jobs in a large house. If you're in one room, or even upstairs, and you want to shut off the power to that outlet from a fuse box in another room (or downstairs), first plug in a radio to that outlet and turn the volume up loud. This will save you a trip back to that room to check on whether the power is indeed off, because when you then go to the fuse box to shut off the power, the radio will shut off when the power does.

Don't Conduct!

Place a rubber mat on the floor under the electric circuit panel, and stand on it whenever touching the panel. This will prevent you from becoming an electricity conductor. Also, always touch the panel with one hand only, while keeping the other in your pocket. If you touch anything else with the other hand, you could become grounded, and thus a current will want to run from the panel and through your body to get to the thing your other hand is touching. This is not good. Note: Always keep a flashlight and a supply of fuses near the electrical panel.

Wrap the Shaft
If you need to use a screwdriver on an electrical job, wrap as much of the shaft as possible with electrical tape. This way, if the shaft accidentally touches another metal object it won't short-circuit your job.

Power Outage
If your power suddenly goes out in a storm, use a flashlight until you're absolutely sure there are no gas leaks. Then and only then you can use a votive candle for light.

Brother, Can You Spare a Fuse?
If you blow a fuse and cannot find a replacement, just "borrow" another fuse from another circuit that is less important until you can replace it with a permanent one.

Cord Coiler
An easy and efficient way to store an extension cord is to convert an old plastic bucket into a "cord coiler." Cut a round hole into the side of the bucket, near the bottom. Feed the pronged end of the cord from the inside of the bucket to the outside, then coil the rest of the cord around and around the inside of the bucket. When you need to use it, just pull it out. It will roll

easily. When you're finished, coil it back into the bucket the same way. This will also be easy, since the cord will now be used to coiling. There will even be space in the middle of the bucket for carrying other tools to a job.

Metal Shavings

If you've just used a saw to file a pipe or other metal object, and you now find metal shavings everywhere, try this: wrap kitchen plastic wrap over a magnet, then pass the magnet over the shavings to pick them up. You can later peel off the plastic into a wastebasket, shavings and all.

Walls, Floors, Windows and Doors

Knuckle Studs

To locate studs in walls without any tools, just use your knuckles. Rap on the wood. If you hear a low-pitched, hollow sound, there's nothing behind the wall. If you hear a higher-pitched, deader sound, you've found the stud. You can also look at the baseboards of the wall for nail holes. Since nails at the top of baseboards (not necessarily the bottoms) are almost always driven into studs, you can just look straight up from there for the studs.

Patch a Large Hole

What if someone in your household got angry and punched a hole in a wall? Or if you were moving furniture and a chair arm accidentally knocked out a big chunk of drywall? No problem. Patching a hole is easy. First, go to your hardware/home improvement store

167

and buy some patching compound. Next, cut out a smooth piece of cloth so that it covers the hole with about two inches to spare all around, then soak it in the compound (which you should first dilute with water for best results). Then smooth the wet cloth over the hole. When it's dry, spread another layer of compound over it (non-diluted), then let that dry. Sand it lightly so that it's now smooth with the wall, then paint it to match the wall.

Patch a Small Hole

This may sound difficult, but it's not. First, cut the hole into a circle, even if it means widening it a little. Then, get a small circular piece of scrap metal, such as the lid of a can, that's a little bigger than the hole. Drill a few small holes into it randomly (about 1/4-inch width) for spackle. Then punch two small holes in the center, and drag about a foot of wire between them. Slide the can lid into the hole. To do this, you will need to cut small slits on each side of the hole. Make sure you hold onto the wires so that the lid doesn't fall behind the wall. Now pull the wire so that the lid is tight against the back of the wall. Straddle a pencil across the hole in the front of the wall, then twist the ends of the wire around it so that the pencil is holding the lid in place. Now spackle the hole. Work around the pencil. Fill the holes in the can lid. But don't fill all the space between the lid and the wall just yet. When the spackle is dry, untie the pencil and snip the wires so that they no longer show. Now spackle again, covering the wire holes and that space you left between the lid and the wall. Stand back and admire your handiwork!

Plunger Patcher

Use a plunger for small plastering jobs. Since most jobs don't require a lot of compound, just mix it in the upside-down plunger, which is handy for transporting and certainly doesn't care what it looks like afterward (although you should wash it anyway).

Vinegar and Plaster

When you mix plastering compound, throw in a little white vinegar—about a tablespoon per pint. This will keep it from drying out so quickly, and won't hurt the quality a bit.

Iron Those Tiles

Ever tried to remove vinyl floor tiles by hand? Sure you have. Lots of pulling, swearing, then cracking of said tiles, until real frustration kicks in. Then you try heating them with the heat gun so the glue on the back dries. Ha ha. You've just burned the surrounding tiles and ruined the subfloor. Yes, there is a better way, and yes, it involves heat. Try this: lay a towel over the tile you want to replace. Now iron it, as you would a shirt—using slow, steady strokes, just like shaving. Now remove the iron and towel, and remove the tile. Simple. Next tile.

Cracked Floor?

Got a cracked floor? A particularly unsightly section of the kitchen floor pattern? Here's what you do. Hopefully, when you installed the flooring you kept some leftover pieces in the garage. No? Okay, then take your patch piece from somewhere it's not needed—say, under the refrigerator. Now cut it into a square or rectangle, making sure it's at least an inch larger than the unsightly area all the way around. Slap it down over the area to be replaced and align with the design on the rest of the floor so it matches aesthetically. Now tape it down with the strongest tape you own. Take a very sharp utility knife with a solid metal straightedge and cut at a right angle exactly one-half inch from the edge of your patch. Yes, this means you're cutting a half-inch into good flooring. Don't worry about it. Remove the tape, remove the patch. Pry out the bad section of flooring and the half-inch perimeter. Now you're patch should fit perfectly. But before you set it in, cut several strips of masking tape and slide them all around the edges, a little under the good flooring, so that the sticky side is up. Now set the patch in. It not only fits perfectly and matches the floor pattern, but the tape holds it firmly in place. Now have your kids stomp all over it.

Squeaky Floors?

No, your house is not haunted. Your wood is just a little dry, so lubricate it. The best way is to just sprinkle talcum powder or furniture wax into the boards adjoining the squeaky one. That way, when the board moves under one's weight, it will be buffered by the lubricant, and thus will not squeak.

Sticky Window

Run a pizza cutter along the groove to loosen any particles that may be holding the window down, such as paint or randomly collected goo. This should free it safely.

Sticky Window II

If the pizza cutter trick fails, you'll have to work a little harder. Find a small wood block and a few screws, and screw it into the bottom sash of the window (of course, you are working on the inside). Now place another small wood block directly underneath it on the window sill. What we're making here is a lever. Now take a long, flat stick and slide it between the two wood blocks, then pry open the window. Believe it or not, it works!

Sticky Window III

If your window opens, but not easily, you may just need to lubricate your vertical tracks. A candle works well for this—just rub it along the inside of the tracks. The wax left behind should be enough to smooth out that friction and ease opening and closing.

Shuffling Windows

A loose window can pose some serious problems to the homeowner—especially on a nice, sunny day. If not fixed, you will eventually be unable to keep the window open. Who wants to sit inside a house with the windows shut on a beautiful spring day? Solving this problem, however, is a snap. To keep it open, simply drill a small hole in the channel in which the window slides up and down. This hole should be big enough to accommodate a nail, without having to use too much force to insert or remove it. Drill the hole just below the bottom of the window when it is open; insert the nail, and it won't fall down anymore. Simply remove the nail when you want to shut it. A bigger problem posed by windows such as this is that they let cold air in the house during the winter, increasing your heating bill. You can prevent this by covering the outside of the window with a thick plastic bag secured with duct tape.

Screen Tips

If the metal screen in your window gets a small tear in it, you don't have to throw it out. Simply glue the torn area back together with a strong bonding epoxy, which can be found at any hardware store. Always read the directions when using glues such as this. To clean your screen (a chore which should be done at least once a year), hose it down and scrub it with a small piece of shag carpeting.

No Window Cleaner?

If you simply must clean your windows and you find that you're plumb out of window cleaner, just pour a cup of cornstarch into a gallon of warm water. Dab it on with a sponge, then dry it with a paper towel. The amazing thing is, it's actually more effective than that ammonia or alcohol-based bottle you pay for at the store, and it's healthier too.

Cracked Window

While waiting to repair a cracked window, dab liquid cement on both sides of the glass, overlapping the crack by a half-inch on each side. This will bond the crack, temporarily preventing it from shattering completely.

Sticky Doors

The easiest method for unsticking a door is to first determine where the door is tightest against either the frame or the floor. Take a dollar bill and try to slide it in between the door and the frame, and the door and the floor, until it's hard to remove. There's your problem area. Once determined, tape sandpaper to the frame (or the floor) at exactly that spot. With regular use, the door will miraculously sand itself down until it no longer sticks. For sliding doors, lubricate the tracks with either graphite or silicone spray. Do not use oil, because it will just accumulate more dirt over time, which just exacerbates your problem. If neither of the above ideas work, you may have a bowed door, which simply means the wood is too old. You can check this by extending a string from the top to the bottom of the frame. If the wood touches the string at its center, it's bowed. Time to replace it.

Banging Door

If your door bangs too loudly when you shut it, you can dampen the sound by gluing 1/8-inch tabs of foam rubber at a few intervals along the part of the frame against which the door shuts. They're flexible enough to allow the door to still shut easily, and yet they add peace and quiet to your hectic life.

The Roof, Attic and Gutters

Safety First

Here's a really safe way of inspecting your roof for leaks: use binoculars or the zoom lens on your camera. This way, you won't ever have to set foot on the roof, as an accidental fall from up there could be life-threatening. This will also save you money when it comes time to call a repairman, as you will be able to point out to him exactly where the problem is, thereby saving him a great deal of time that would be passed over to you in the bill.

Aged Shingles

If you need to replace old shingles with new ones and you don't want the new ones to stand out visually, you can make them look older. Just mix one pound

173

baking soda with a half gallon of water, then brush or spray the solution onto the shingles. After a few hours, they'll look suitably gray.

Mildewed Shingles

To rid your roof shingles of mildew, scrub them with either straight vinegar or a solution of half bleach and half water. Once clean, coat them twice with wood sealant. This can also apply to other wooden exteriors, such as decks, fences or sheds.

Melted Snow

Does your attic need more insulation? A good way to check, if you live in a northern climate, is to walk outside a few hours after a snowfall. If the snow is melting in a certain spot on the roof more than in others, that's because heat is escaping there. If heat is escaping, your house will be colder and require more energy to be heated. You'll need to refurbish the insulation in those spots.

Attic Insulation

Attic insulation is most commonly laid in between those big ceiling beams, or joists. Check to make sure the insulation is thorough, and level with the top of the joists. If you want to add more, it's best to lay it across the first layer of insulation at a right angle, to absolutely minimize the potential of any heat escaping.

Gutter Gadgets

If you live in an area where the trees shed their leaves each autumn, then you're probably familiar with the problem of dead leaves clogging up your gutter. This problem can lead to serious damage to the down

174

spout, not to mention the water damage the side of your house can receive if the gutter overflows. A great way to prevent this is to use a leaf strainer, an ingenious little gadget that fits at the top of your down spout. But remember to clean the strainer fairly regularly, as it will be useless if you allow it to get clogged up with leaves.

Clogged Gutter

You can also prevent leaves and other debris from clogging your gutters by covering the tops with a hardware cloth, or mesh screen. Make sure the screen's opening does not exceed 3/8 of an inch. This way, the gutter can do its job more efficiently by letting in rain water, not leaves.

Clean Gutter

The best way to clean a gutter is with a plumber's snake. Work your way up from the bottom, so that as you plow through the gutter, leaves and other detritus fall out naturally. For the higher, hard-to-reach section, run a garden hose up the gutter and turn it on all the way, so that the water forces the debris out.

Sagging Gutter

If your roof gutter is sagging, you can pitch it back to level just by tightening its strap with pliers. The tighter you twist it, the more the gutter will rise.

Downspout

At the bottom of your gutter, add a three-foot downspout that extends outward from your house. This way, rain water will not empty directly alongside your house, causing potential damage. Even better, drill a few small holes in the new downspout, so that the water empties out in small rivulets all around, covering a much wider area and keeping your house safe and dry.

Saving Energy, Money and Lives

You might not want to admit it, but right now you are probably wasting a tremendous amount of energy throughout your house. For example, rather than putting on another layer of clothing, did you turn the heater up? Have you resorted to using the air conditioner when closing the blinds might have cooled down the house?

This chapter will give you a few hints on reducing your energy bills, and even lessening the amount of pollution in the world too! Aside from doing your part to save Mother Earth, you will also learn a little about saving yourself. The few tips presented below can introduce you to the hazards which may be lurking in your household. For example, do you know what kind of items should be kept in a natural disaster survival kit? Do you know how to keep from tripping down the stairs at night when it's dark? You'll soon learn how!

Climate Control
Lower Temperature
Adjust the temperature on your hot water heater. Most are set at 140 degrees, which is far too hot for most people. You'll save lots of energy and money by setting it lower—such as at 120 degrees, which is still plenty hot.

Leaving Town?
If you plan to leave home for a few days, turn off your water heater altogether to save even more money. In fact, you can purchase a thermostat that will do this for you automatically every day when you're not using it—it will shut off at night and turn on in the morn-

ing, just before you awake. The small investment in the thermostat will pay great dividends on your monthly energy bill.

Drain Your Heater

Drain your water heater every four to six months to rid it of sedimentary deposits. This will help it run more efficiently, and again, save you money.

Save Your Bathwater!

In the wintertime, leave the water in the bathtub for a while after you've finished bathing. Since the water is still warm, it will release heat into the air, thus helping heat your home. It will also add humidity to the air, which is important to homes which have a problem with dry air in the wintertime.

Hot Aluminum

Remember how you learned to use aluminum foil as a kind of "double iron" in the chapter on laundry? Well, the same concept can be used to save energy with heaters. If you place sheets of heavy grade aluminum foil behind your radiator, then you can angle them in such a way as to ensure that more heat is reflected into the room, thereby utilizing the energy more efficiently and saving you money.

The Magic of Blinds

Do you know how a greenhouse works? The concept is very simple: all the panes of glass let rays of light into the structure, which subsequently get trapped inside and raise the temperature. How can you use this greenhouse effect to your advantage? In the summer you should keep your curtains or blinds shut during the day, so that the sunlight will be kept out.

179

That way, you won't have to turn the air conditioning so high. In the winter, you should leave the blinds or curtains open, so that sunlight can enter your house and warm it up. This will reduce your heating bill.

Shut the Door!

This tip is simple yet highly effective. Keep all doors within the house closed while using either air conditioning or heating. This will prevent the warm air or cool air from drifting into unused areas. With the climate control being used more efficiently, you can turn it to a lower setting, thereby saving you money.

Water Conservation

New Shower Head

One of the greatest new advances in plumbing is the water-conservation shower head. This remarkable new device will save you a considerable amount of money each month by dramatically reducing the amount of water that it sprays. If you're worried that you won't feel as refreshed as you would with a normal shower head, however, then you should lay your fears to rest. By increasing the amount of air that mixes with the water in the spray, you'll hardly notice any difference at all. These heads are even quite inexpensive, and very easy to install!

Not so Tight!

This might surprise you, but one of the worst ways to try and save water is by twisting your faucets very tight when you turn them off. When you do that, all that happens is that you crush the gasket in the faucet, thereby ruining the water tight seal. Over time, the seal deteriorates to such a point that the faucet inevitably becomes leaky, dripping all night long! You'd be amazed at how much a leaky faucet can add to your water bill. So just remember, not too tight.

No Baths, Please

Many people are under the impression that baths use less water than showers, but this couldn't be farther from the truth. If you are conscientious and have quick showers, then you will use much less water. If you find this difficult to believe, then try filling up your bathtub with individual buckets of water; you'll be amazed at how many buckets it takes to fill it up. If you do decide to have a bath, however, there is a way that you can use its energy to your advantage. In winter, when things are chilly, leave the tub filled after having your bath. It will stay relatively hot for about an hour, and this heat will help to raise the temperature of your house!

Recycling

Cans and Bottles

If your family goes through lots of soda pop or beer, then you should start saving the used cans and bottles. Whenever convenient, take them to a local supermarket with recycling machines. Recycling not only helps out the environment, it helps out your pocket book too. The redemption value for bottles and cans varies from state to state, but it is usually around a nickel. If you save all of the change that you collect from recycling in a jar, after a few months you'll have enough money to treat your family to something special!

Newspaper

It's wonderful to get the morning paper each day and read it over a hot cup of coffee. But after that, there isn't really any place to put it (if you're like most people, then your garage has a whole year's worth of newspapers stacked up in the corner). Well, now that you're getting your place organized, isn't it about time that you took it to the nearest recycling center? Although not all centers pay you for your used newspaper, at the very least you're getting a pile of junk out of your otherwise neat house. You'll also be helping in the crusade to save the environment, something from which we can all benefit.

Recycled Paper

If you have a home office, then chances are you do a lot of paperwork each day. But instead of using good quality cotton bond paper for every document you produce, why not use recycled white paper whenever you can. Not only is it much cheaper (sometimes you can get it for about one-fifth the price of bond paper, if you buy it in bulk!), but it is also much better for the environment. You should at least consider using it for all your rough drafts. And speaking of rough drafts, remember to print on both sides of the paper whenever possible.

Budgeting

Plan for the Month

Organizing your bank book is as important as organizing your home. You should set up strict budgets for yourself, and not stray from those budgets. That way, you will force yourself to be on alert for the best bargains. It is probably best to budget out your money for an entire month, rather than for just one week or two. The reason for this is that many items, particularly food and sanitary products, are very cheap when bought in bulk; you will pay much less by buying meat for a month than by buying it for a week. One important category to never leave off of any budget: savings!

Three Months

How much money should you save? This is the question that most people torment themselves with for hours and hours. Many money experts believe that the minimum savings you should have is three months worth of your salary in liquid assets; that is, money that is readily available. Why three months? Let's face it, horrible things can happen at any moment. Three months worth of money should be enough for you to live on if you happen to lose your job, or if you get hospitalized.

Bills

You should keep a file that you go through at least once a week for your bills. You should never leave paying a bill until the last minute, in case your payment gets lost in the mail. Likewise, you shouldn't pay a bill too early, or you will lose the interest on your money that you could have accrued. Try to pay each bill about seven days before it is due. Once you have sent your payment, file the bill in a file just for that type of bill. Then, when it comes time to file your taxes at the end of the year, they will already be sorted into the correct category for you.

Car Care

In this hectic day and age, your car should be considered part of your household. After all, it's just as indispensable as the roof over your head. As such, your household budget should include its maintenance. While such costs vary from car to car, you should be prepared to pay for at least two major servicings per year, two minor servicings (such as oil changes), and at least one regrettable mishap (like needing a new tire). In order to make a good estimate for your car, read your warranty and find out what parts are covered. Ask your dealer for the prices of labor and commonly needed parts that aren't covered.

Be Realistic

The best advice that anyone can get regarding their budget is to be realistic. Don't trick yourself into thinking that a family of four can be fed for $20 a month, because even the best shopper can't find bargains like that. Making a budget that is too tight is like making an impossible New Year's resolution, so save yourself some grief. If anything, you should *overestimate* your spending; anything that you don't actually spend can go into your savings.

Home Safety

Emergency Kit

In the last decade, various parts of the country have been ravaged by natural disasters. Whether it's earthquakes in California or flooding along the Mississippi, nature has certainly exerted its dominion over mankind. The key to fighting such disasters is to be prepared. Emergency kits obviously must vary depending upon the disasters that threaten your region of the country; a raft is more important along the Mississippi than it is in Los Angeles, for example. There are certain constants, however. For example, all kits must have radios and flashlights *with fresh batteries*. All kits should have sterile bandages and antiseptics, dried food rations, and several gallons of purified drinking water. Consult emergency officials in your neighborhood for the exact contents necessary in your region. *No house can ever truly be considered organized without an emergency kit.*

Smoke Detectors

Smoke detectors are inexpensive and they can save your life. If you don't already have several in your home, then go out and buy them. If you do already have some in your home, make sure that they are installed correctly and that the batteries are fresh. You should change the batteries at least twice a year. Professionals recommend that you change them when you set your clocks forward or back; that way, you won't forget. Incidentally, that would probably also be a good time to change the batteries in your emergency kit.

Chemicals and Drugs

Kids are naturally curious, and unfortunately they seem to gravitate toward things that aren't good for them. We all keep hazardous chemicals and prescription drugs around the house, so they must be stored away properly. Always put chemicals, such as cleansing products, on the highest shelves, where they can't be reached by children. You might even want to consider locking them up. You have already learned that drugs should not be stored in the bathroom, so that eliminates the chance of kids finding them in the medicine cabinet. But you shouldn't just leave them lying around in your bedroom, in case your child stumbles upon them; hide them someplace safe!

Sharp Idea

Here's a good way not to cut yourself on the tips of knives that are in drawers: insert them into corks. This will reduce your chance of injury whenever you grab for a knife. This is especially important in households with kids.

Electricity

Have you ever noticed those special electrical outlets they have in hotel bathrooms with the little button on them. This button is a miniature circuit breaker. It cuts the flow of electricity off in the event that you drop a hairdryer or electric shaver into a sink or bathtub filled with water. Most of us aren't lucky enough to have such sophisticated outlets, but we all have fuse boxes in our basements or garages. If you ever drop your hairdryer in the sink, don't touch, or even try to pull the cord out of the wall! *Go down and turn off the fuse corresponding to the outlet in which the appliance is plugged!* Once you have done this, no more electricity is surging through it, so it is safe to touch. Unplug it, drain the water, and let it dry thoroughly before trying to use it again. An even simpler solution is to always drain the water *before* using a hairdryer or shaver.

Toasted Fingers

Toasters are so easy to use that you probably wouldn't even think twice about letting your youngest child use one. But don't forget, they do carry a large current of energy through them and, as such, can be very dangerous. If a piece of toast ever gets stuck inside, then the first thing you should do is *unplug the appliance.* Then, use a wooden instrument to remove it. Never use your fingers or any metal object, or you run a very high risk of suffering an electrical shock.

Vacation Security

If you are going away on vacation, then you want to make sure your home is safe while you are away. There are professional services which will look after your house, but this can be expensive. Instead, just ask a neighbor to take care of it for you; you will save yourself a lot of money (the only form of payment you might have to make is repaying the favor). Your neighbor should visit your home every day and turn different lights on and off. He or she should open the curtains in the morning and close them at night. He or she should collect your mail and your newspaper, and possibly even take care of your lawn. The idea is to make sure that no burglar would ever suspect that your house is empty.

Burned Batteries

We all know the feeling of reaching for a flashlight and turning it on . . . only to find that nothing happens. When you open it up, you discover that the batteries are so old that they've actually started to melt and the acid is dripping out, destroying the inside of your flashlight. There is no way to prevent this from happening to any battery operated appliance. The only thing you can do is change your batteries on a regular basis, so that nothing gets damaged and everything functions when needed.

Stair Cases

Stair cases can be remarkably dangerous, especially to kids and the elderly. You should always do your best to draw attention to the first and last steps of any staircase, so that eyes cannot be distracted away from them, especially in dark places. The most efficient way to do this is to cover the first and last steps of your cellar stair case with fluorescent tape.

187

Glass

We all keep a great deal of glass products in the kitchen and bathroom. Unfortunately, these types of rooms usually have hard tile floors, meaning that if anything made of glass gets dropped, then it will probably break. Those tiny little shards are so hard to find! To make your search easier, turn off the main lights and shine a flashlight on the ground. The shards will identify themselves by reflecting the flashlight beam.

No More Bacteria

Bacteria can be one of the most dangerous threats in your house. But if you know how to handle foods correctly, then you need not worry. First, you should clean your can opener thoroughly at least once a week. Don't just wash it off with water, but scrub it with baking soda. Second, if you ever open a can and hear a loud hissing noise, then *throw out the contents of the can immediately! They have been tainted while still on the shelf!* Finally, in the event of a power outage, resist the urge to open your refrigerator or freezer to make sure your food is okay. If you leave them shut, your food will stay cool for several hours, which is usually enough time for the electricity to return. If, however, the power takes a long time to come back and your frozen foods thaw out, then you will have to throw them out. *Never* refreeze them.

Bright Ideas

Most people always seem to forget where they put the flashlight when there's a power outage. A good way to help you find useful items such as these in the dark is to wrap them in fluorescent tape. This can also be helpful on light switches and light cords if you have to get up suddenly in the middle of the night. Also, if a fuse ever blows, have a spare one already attached to the side of the box with tape, so that you'll always be able to turn the lights back on in a jiffy.

Life Saving Alarm

If your home doesn't already have a smoke detector on every floor, then go out and buy some. They are quite inexpensive, and if a tragedy ever hits your home, then they could be responsible for saving your life. If you already have one or two installed in your home, then you should clean them out regularly. As air has to be able to flow in and out of them with ease, dust tends to get caught in their vents. This then prevents the alarm from detecting the smoke! All you need to do is brush out the dust or suck it up with your vacuum cleaner. You should also make a rigid schedule for testing the alarm's batteries, conducting a check every three to four weeks.

Time Delay

Most of us shut off lights, then have to stumble around in the dark for a few seconds until we reach where we're going. There is a solution. Purchase a time delay switch, so that after turning a light off, it remains on for 30, 45, or 60 seconds longer, allowing you to find your way without bumping your shin against the coffee table.

See-Saw Switch

Ever walk into a dark house with your arms full of groceries, then try to turn on the light switch? It's not pretty. Solve this problem by installing a "see-saw" switch. It extends out a little farther, allowing you to move it up or down with just an elbow or shoulder.

Glow-in-the-Dark Switch

Ever have trouble *finding* the light switch in the dark? We've all entered a guest's dark bathroom, only to then blindly feel around the walls for a switch. This is also unsafe—you could knock something over, which then crashes on top of you and makes an embarrassing noise. Solve this problem by installing (or convincing your friend to install) a switch with an illuminated lever.

Your Automobile

Would you ever sit down to write a letter if you did not have a pencil and a piece of paper? Would you ever try to build a piece of furniture without the proper tools? Of course not, so why would you try to wash your car without preparing yourself correctly? Washing a car, like writing a letter or building a piece of furniture, is a process. And, as with all processes, there is a right way and a wrong way to go about doing it.

The wrong way goes something like this. You set aside a half an hour every six months or so and splash water all over your car while it is parked in the driveway. Needless to say, the results of your labor are far from stunning, so you pick up an old brush that you found in the back of your garage and do a little scrubbing. Uh-oh! You just gouged a great big scratch into your car's finish! In trying to clean your car, you've actually created permanent damage.

Now, let's take a look at the right way.

Take a good look at your car. Where is it dirty? If the inside is still clean as button, then don't waste your time washing it. If the outside still sparkles like new, then concentrate solely on the interior. As you will see in the pages that follow, the best way to clean a car is to provide continual attention to it throughout the year, rather than simply washing it all at once every now and then. You should make notes on this chapter as you read it, so that you can create a schedule of cleaning chores for yourself. This week you will wash the tires, two weeks from now you will empty out the ashtrays, etc. You should then leave the schedule in your glove compartment or some other convenient location. That way, whenever you get stuck in traffic, you can make good use of your idle time by reviewing the schedule! The great thing about schedules is that they allow you to budget your time correctly. As a result, you will never have to spend more than a few minutes per week attending to your car.

In order to take proper care of your automobile, you will need to keep some basic supplies on-hand. What follows is a list of items you will need, along with some basic explanations for their uses. And remember to clear out a special area in your garage in which to keep these supplies.

1. Bucket: A bucket is a must. Naturally, this is used for carrying around large amounts of water. Buckets are also useful because you can put other items inside them when they are not in use.

2. Hose: You can't give your car a really good wash unless you have a hose. If possible, try to get your hands on one of those spray-gun hose heads. They provide more pressure than just using a hose alone, and they also prevent you from wasting water.

3. An assortment of rags: Old T-Shirts often make the best rags, because they are generally made out of soft and cushy cotton. If you prefer you can go out and buy new rags, but the old shirts will probably do the trick.

4. Chamois: A chamois, or shammy, is a special type of rag made out of extremely soft fabric. It is used during the final stages of cleaning your car, when you are going around trying to get any spots that you missed (which is an inevitable occurrence). A shirt cannot be substituted for a shammy. Shammy's are

often chemically treated so that dust clings more easily to them.

5. Soap: Probably the best type of soap you can use for cleaning your car is dishwashing soap. This is due to the mild nature of this kind of cleanser. Most other soaps contain far greater amounts of acid, which could eventually eat away at your car's finish!

6. Tire cleansers: You can buy special detergents made especially for getting the dirt off tires, and this might be necessary if you haven't cleaned them in a long time. These detergents also make the rubber shine like new.

7. Brushes: You should have a wide assortment of brushes at hand, all of which have extremely soft and gentle bristles. Small brushes, like old toothbrushes, can be used to scrub dirt out of tiny areas. Larger brushes can be used to lather up soap on broad surfaces like your car's hood.

8. A knife: A somewhat dull knife, such as a butter knife, is often good to have around. You can use it to pop little pebbles out of the grooves in your tires. Make sure that the knife is dull enough to prevent you from cutting yourself if you slip. If you prefer, you could also try using a Popsicle stick.

9. Vinyl/leather cleaner: If your car has vinyl or leather seats, then this item is essential. There is no way to restore vinyl or leather to its original glossy sheen unless you use this type of product.

10. Stain remover: If your car has cloth seats, then you can use conventional furniture stain remover to get

out any pesky stains. Be sure to follow the directions carefully, or you might accidentally bleach some of the die out of the seat.

11. Silicone spray: This item is used to keep rubber from getting cracked and brittle, such as the seals around your windows. These products should always be used with caution, as their fumes are unhealthy. Never begin applying a coat of silicone spray without first reading the instructions.

12. Vacuum: Cars need to be vacuumed on a fairly regular basis. It is best to either use a vacuum that has a long hose, or to use one of those small handheld models. It is my belief, however, that the cleaners with hoses do a far better job.

13. Aerosol disinfectant: This is great for spraying out ashtrays, as well as for removing any foul odors from the interior of your car.

14. Tar removing cleanser: This detergent is specifically designed to get sticky tar spots from highways and roads off of your car.

15. Polish: This is the agent that gives your car's paint job a showroom shine.

16. Wax: This agent coats your car's paint job, protecting it from the elements.

17. Buffing pad: The powder puff shaped applicator for polish.

18. Touch-up paint: Small chips in your car's paint job can be touched up with this paint.

Interior

General Clutter

Many people keep their car's interior in a state of disarray. This is not only inconvenient, as it greatly reduces the amount of cabin space that you have available to passengers, but it is also very dangerous. You see, if you ever get into an accident, your car comes to a sudden stop. If you were traveling at 50 miles per hour prior to the accident, then everything inside the car will continue to travel at that speed after the car has come to a halt. As you probably know, if you don't wear a seat belt, then there is a great chance that you can be thrown through the front windshield. Any loose items will also be thrown around, and scientists have estimated that being struck in the back of the head with a hardcover book that was in the car during a serious accident is just about as lethal as being shot in the back of the head with a bullet! So it is no joke that your car should be kept as clutter free as possible. Therefore, whenever you clean out your car, be sure to remove anything that you don't need. After all, your car can't look as clean as new if there is a lot of junk littering the seats and floors.

Vinyl Dashboards

The top of the dashboard of almost every car on the road today is made out of some kind of vinyl. Auto manufacturers probably have a good reason for choosing this material (perhaps it reduces glare on the windshield), but it is terribly difficult to keep looking like new, especially if you live in an area with a warm climate. Direct sunlight on this material will make it start to crack and wither. As such, it might be a good idea for you to buy one of those fabric dashboard covers, which can easily be cleaned with a vacuum cleaner. If you prefer not to purchase one of these items, then you should make sure to pay special attention to your dashboard. Clean it every few weeks with soap and warm water, and after each cleaning give it a good rub down with a vinyl treatment that can be purchased at most drug stores. This will keep the vinyl moist and help prevent it from cracking.

Leather Seats

All of us love the feeling of supple leather supporting our bodies when we are on a long drive, and a few of us are fortunate enough to possess such a luxury in our cars. But leather, like vinyl, is especially susceptible to the sun's harmful rays, and should therefore be attended to on a regular basis. Wash your seats with a mixture of soap and warm water every other week, and then massage in a good coating of saddle soap or other leather treatment product. Such products are easy to find in auto specialty stores, drug stores, and sometimes even supermarkets. Many people like to wax their leather to give it extra shine, but this only amplifies the damage caused by the sun!

Cloth Seats

Cloth seats, while not as wonderful as leather seats, are in many ways much easier to keep clean. You can often get away with simply vacuuming them every few weeks to remove any small particles and debris that may be on them. This is especially true if you have kids; it is always better to remove dirt before it has the chance to get rubbed into the seat and become a stain. Many car manufacturers these days are even making their seat fabrics stain proof, so you might want to consider this option when you are purchasing your next car. If dirt does become a stain, then you will have to prepare yourself for some work. First, you should shampoo your seats with soap and warm water, to get them as fresh as possible. Then you will need to treat the area with the stain with a store-bought stain remover. Usually these detergents work on specific types of stains, so you will have to select the correct one. They can be found in drug stores or grocery stores. You should follow the directions on the package of stain remover carefully, so as not to tear the fabric on the seat. Usually, the remover will tell you to scrub with a firm yet gentle brush. If you do not have such a brush, then you should purchase one while buying the remover.

Steering Wheel, Etc.

Your car's interior has many parts in it that are made of a rigid plastic. Examples of these parts include the steering wheel, the stick shifter knob, and the manual window levers. Like the soft vinyl of your dashboard, these can get damaged over time by the rays of the sun. If you live in an especially hot climate, then you might want to consider buying one of those fuzzy steering wheel covers. This will also make it easier for you to touch the steering wheel when first entering the car on a very hot day. To keep these plastic items looking like new, you should wash them every month or so with soap and warm water. For a really bright finish, you can even apply a coating furniture polish.

Floor Mats

Floor mats are probably the easiest things in your car to keep clean. This is because they have been very sensibly designed by car manufactures. All you have to do is remove them from your automobile and spray them down with a hose. If that doesn't get all the dirt out, then you can scrub them with soap and warm water. Make sure to rinse any soap off thoroughly, or the soap will dry and make the rubber brittle. You should try to hang up your mats to dry, so they don't leave any drip marks. If you have a laundry line in your back yard, then this is the perfect place to do it. Store-bought tire cleaner can then be applied, and this will make your floor mats sparkle even more brilliantly than when they were new.

Carpets

Underneath the floor mats, most cars have a layer of carpeting. If you clean your floor mats on a regular basis, then you can simply spend an extra few minutes vacuuming the carpeting to get it clean. Pick up any larger items with your hands first, however, as they could get stuck in the hose of your vacuum cleaner (and this could be quite expensive to repair or replace). You will probably find a dollar or more in change if you haven't done this for a while, so you should go out and treat yourself to some ice cream as a reward for cleaning your car! If your carpets are very dirty or stained, then you should clean them with a store-bought rug shampoo. Simply follow the directions on the packaging. You should make sure that the carpets are thoroughly dried before you put the floor mats in again, or the wet fibers will trap the dirt from the soles of your shoes even more easily! You should probably let the carpet dry overnight, if possible. Be sure to leave the windows open when drying, or your car will smell like mildew.

Metal

Many of today's finer cars are going for a retro look; that is, you will often see cars that have metallic pieces exposed. Examples include the manual window levers, the stick shifter, and the rims around your dashboard's instrument gauges. The secret to keeping these parts looking like new is to wipe them clean with a soft cloth every week or so. That way, fingerprints and smudges can be removed easily, without having to resort to cleansers that can harm the metal. If it has been a while since you last cleaned these metal surfaces, then you should wipe them with warm water. Do not use soap or detergent of any kind, as they will permanently rob the metal of its luster!

Sun Visors

The sun visors in most cars are made out of a metal frame with a soft vinyl material covering it. This vinyl, like the top of your dashboard, is very susceptible to the sun (so why car makers have chosen this as the material for their sun guards is beyond me!). The best way to keep them looking like new and prevent them from fading is to not use them at all. Why not just keep a pair of sunglasses in the car, so that you can put them on on bright days? There's really nothing you can do to remove that awful yellow-bleached color from the sun visor once it sets in.

Windows

Everyone has some method for washing their car's windows that a long-lost uncle once taught them. But the fact of the matter is, there is only one sure fire way of cleaning any glass without streaks. Get a store-bought window cleaner and spray it onto the glass. Then lightly crumple up a newspaper and wipe off the cleanser with slow and even circular motions. No one is really sure why newspaper works the best, and scientists have even conducted a few studies to try and figure out why. If you are skeptical about the advantages of newspaper, then test it out for yourself.

Spray your windscreen with a store-bought glass cleaner, and then wipe off small areas with different types of material (i.e., cloth, regular paper, paper towels, newspaper, etc.). I guarantee you that the area you wiped with newspaper will have the least amount of streaks! Once you've cleaned the glass itself, you should take a look at the rubber seals around the window. Rubber is literally eaten away by the sun, so chances are your seals are worn and cracked. This is just the kind of detail that betrays a car's true age, so if you really want your car looking brand new, then you might want to invest a few bucks and have these seals replaced. If you just want them to look as nice as possible, then treat them with a silicone spray. These sprays can be harmful if used incorrectly, however, so read the directions carefully.

Rear View Mirrors
One of the most important safety items you have with you inside the passenger compartment of your car is the rear view mirror. As such, you owe it to yourself, as well as to your passengers, to keep the mirror clean and free of clutter. First of all, don't hang any ornaments from the mirror. Not only can they make the car's interior seem less tidy and obscure your view of the mirror, but they are also illegal in many states! So if you have a pair of fuzzy dice hanging down in front of you, then you might be breaking the law depending on where you live. The glass of the mirror should be cleaned in exactly the same way as your windows. Apply a window cleaner with a piece of loosely crumpled newspaper. If you haven't cleaned it in a long time, then you will be surprised at how much more clearly and brightly you can see objects in the mirror.

Pedals

Most pedals are made out of metal and have a rubber covering on them. The rubber piece usually comes off very easily. To clean the metal, simply wipe it with a soft cloth that has been dipped in warm water. To clean the rubber pieces, simply soak them in a bucket of soap and warm water for a few hours. Then buff them up with a coating of tire cleaner. Your car might have an area called a "dead pedal," which is a rubber foot rest for your left foot. You should also wash this with soap and warm water, and then apply the tire cleaner. If you have lost any of the rubber pedal covers, then you should have them replaced. They are not merely for cosmetic value, but are also to provide friction between your foot and the pedal. If the soles of your shoes are wet, then they could very easily slip off the bare metal!

Glove Compartment

I don't think I have ever known anyone who keeps their car's glove compartment tidy and well organized. But this is such a wonderful storage area, why should you waste it by cluttering it up with junk that you don't need? When you take the time to wash your car, you should certainly spend a few minutes attending to the glove compartment. The only things that should be inside are your car's registration and insurance documentation, any necessary maps, and any small tools or emergency supplies that might come in handy. Bottles of nail polish, the sports pages, and pieces of gum should all be left outside the car!

Smells

The best way to keep your car smelling like new is to prevent any smells from becoming trapped inside in the first place. This means you should drive with your windows open whenever possible (this will also help increase your gas mileage, as you won't be able to turn on the air conditioner). You should also avoid smoking inside your car. Cleaning out your car on a regular basis will also help keep it smelling fresh. And most importantly of all, make sure your window seals are still tight and secure. If they are not, then water will slowly seep inside your car on rainy days, filling the interior with a mildewy smell. If your car does have a foul odor that you can't seem to get rid of, then you can buy several types of odor removers from most auto supply stores. These are extremely potent formulas, and a few drops is all it takes to keep your car smelling new for weeks on end. Be careful not to spill any on your clothes, or they will smell like a pine forest for years! It might also be a good idea to place a conventional air freshener under one of the front seats and replace it whenever necessary.

Ashtrays

While we are on the topic of smells, we should also discuss ashtrays. As mentioned in the entry above, cigarette smoking is a prime culprit for making your car smelly. Thus, if you do choose to smoke inside your vehicle, you owe it to yourself to clean out your ashtrays at least every two weeks. And by cleaning them out, I don't just mean emptying them of cigarette butts (which you should do at least twice a week). I mean that you should actually take them and dunk them in a bucket of warm, soapy water. You might even want to spray them with a bit of aerosol disinfectant. While you have the can of aerosol out, you should also spray some around the rest of the car's interior.

The Trunk

Let's face it, even if we treat our cars really well, cleaning and maintaining them as often as we should, chances are we still don't take enough care of our trunk. Most people's trunks look more like garbage cans than like storage areas! The first thing you should do is empty out everything inside your trunk. Anything that doesn't need to be in there should be put in its proper place. Any junk should be thrown away. This is an excellent opportunity for you to check out your spare tire. Most people's spares are flat, which doesn't help much when you actually have to change your tire. Hose off your spare tire and then clean it with store-bought tire cleaner. Also make sure that you still have your jack. If you don't, then your newly filled spare tire will be useless. If the base of your trunk is made out of rubber, then it should be washed off with soap and warm water. You shouldn't have to use any silicone spray, as sunlight rarely penetrates your trunk. If the base is made out of carpeting, then you should vacuum it on a regular basis. You should also wash it with soap and warm water at least twice a year. To keep a mildew smell from occurring within the trunk, you should keep it open while drying. It is also a good idea to stick a small air freshener in one corner of the trunk and replace it whenever necessary.

The Engine

Most people don't consider the engine compartment to be the interior of their car, but it is a space *inside* the outer body. Moreover, it should be cleaned. Why should you take the time to clean the engine? Because doing so will decrease the chances of pieces of dirt, twigs, dust, and other floating debris of penetrating your engine and causing serious damage. In fact, many top mechanics believe that keeping an engine clean is one of the best and most simple measures of preventative maintenance you can take. And if you want to make a mechanic happy (and who doesn't, considering that a happy mechanic might be able to lower the cost of your repair bill?!), then you will never pull into a garage and ask him to take a look at a dirty engine. Essentially, all you have to do to keep your engine clean is to hose it down every now and then. But you do have to take a little bit of care not to get anything wet that shouldn't be. First, you should either remove the battery or cover it securely with a leakproof plastic bag. Removing a battery is usually not very difficult, but consult your car's owner's manual before attempting this, in case there are any details of which you need to be aware. Then, using the manual as a guide, locate all of the spark plugs and the distributor. These items should be covered as tightly as possible with plastic bags—rubber bands usually work well to hold the bags in place. You should also take a few moments to remove any leaves or twigs that have accumulated in the grooves along the outside of your engine compartment. You can now take a hose and *gently* spray down the engine compartment. Don't use too much pressure, or you will blow off the plastic bags you worked so hard to put into place. You should then apply a store-bought engine cleanser. Depending on the cleanser you buy, you might have to rinse it off with soapy water. Once you have done so, you will be amazed at how clean your engine looks!

Seat Belts

The fabric part of your seat belt can be cleaned easily with a vacuum cleaner. The metal buckles require slightly more attention. You read earlier in this chapter that metal pieces should be cleaned on a weekly basis with a dry soft cloth. This holds true for the buckles. But you also need to make sure that no dirt has worked its way inside the clasp, preventing the buckle from being fully inserted. The best way to do this is to spray compressed air into the clasp. Compressed air, which comes in bottles, should always be handled with great care, as you can accidentally release a sticky fluid, which is used as the compressing agents. As long as you follow the directions closely, you shouldn't have any problems. I cannot stress to you enough the importance of keeping your seat belt buckles clean. Because if your seat belt won't fasten properly because of a piece of dirt, then you are putting yourself in grave danger while you are on the road. You probably won't need to do this more than once or twice per year.

The Details

Probably the most important thing for you to remember about keeping your car looking like new is that you have to pay attention to the details. Think back to the last time you visited a new car showroom. If you had the opportunity to sit inside one of the cars, did you take a good look around inside it? Chances are you didn't see any dust lining the seat belt buckles. Likewise, there probably weren't any sticky fingerprints on the steering wheel or on the gearshift knob. And, of course, the vehicle had that famed "new car smell." All it takes is a little effort from you on a regular basis for your car's interior to retain all of the sparkle and sheen it had on the first day you bought it. This kind of attention will not only give you more pleasure out of your car, but it will also guarantee a higher resale value when the time comes for you to part with it.

Exterior

Tires

Tires are one of the most important components of your car. Manufacturers realize this, so tires that are more expensive in price always look nicer too. Well, no matter how expensive or inexpensive the tires are that your car is wearing, they will always look terrible if they are covered in mud and grease. The most basic way to clean a tire is to simply hose it down. If you do this on a fairly regular basis, then the pressure of the water from the hose will remove almost any dirt that gets lodged in the treads. If it's been a while since you last cleaned your tires, then you should get down on your hands and knees and give them a good scrub with soap and warm water. You might want to keep a popsicle stick or butter knife handy, so that you can dislodge any pesky pebbles that have worked their way into the treads. The final stage to cleaning a tire is applying store-bought tire cleanser. This step isn't really essential, but it will add that extra touch of class that a normal car wash can't provide. If your car has whitewall tires (tires with a white stripe running around them), then you can even buy a special cleanser just for the white area.

Wheels

As well as cleaning your tires, you should pay special care to your car's wheels. In the olden days, car wheels were almost as simple as the wheels on your bicycle, but those days are long gone! Manufacturers now realize that wheels are one of the fanciest elements of your car's look. Most car makers offer a variety of different style wheels as options for new car buyers. Many people even like to customize their vehicles by purchasing special wheels called "rims." Rims are beautifully detailed wheels that look much like those found on actual race cars, and they are very expensive. Only a few companies in the world make these products. But even if your budget does not allow for any fancy luxuries like rims, you can still make your car look its best by keeping your wheels and hub caps sparkling clean. A hose will usually not do the trick, even if you clean the car on a regular basis, so be prepared to get down and dirty with a bucket of soap and warm water. You might need to use a small brush to get inside any nooks and crannies where dirt can easily hide, but be sure that the bristles are not too hard. Otherwise, you might scratch the wheel and increase its chances of rusting. If you do have a special hub cap or rim, then consult the manufacturer about the best way to keep it clean. There are many fine products available in auto specialty stores, but the finish on your particular set of wheels might require you to use a certain type of cleanser. Remember, items like rims will make your car that much more beautiful to look at, but they also require that much more care and attention.

Windows

As mentioned in the section on the interior of your car, the best way to clean your windows without leaving streaks is to use glass cleaner that is applied with a piece of crumpled up newspaper. But since the outside of your windshield accumulates far more dirt than the insides do—aren't all of those squished bugs and bird droppings disgusting?—it's probably a good idea to spend a few minutes hosing them down first. Turn the pressure up as high as possible on the hose, so that you can literally force the dirt off. But before you do so, squirt water from the hose softly onto the windows. This way you can judge for yourself whether the rubber seals around the windows are still in good enough condition to keep a hard spray of water out of your car. It would be terrible for you to accidentally soak the driver's seat!

Side View Mirrors
Side view mirrors are cleaned in exactly the same way as rear view mirrors. That is, apply glass cleaner with a crumpled up piece of newspaper. Your side view mirrors should always be kept clean to give you added visibility when making a lane change. Many people find it convenient to clean them with the window cleaners available at service stations while their cars are being filled up with gas.

Windshield Wipers
If you live in a climate where there is a great deal of rain or snow, then you know how vital it is to have clear visibility through your windshield. All of us, at one time or another, have probably driven in the rain. When we went to turn on our windshield wipers, the wiper blades were in such poor condition that they left horrible streaks across the windshield, making it even more difficult to see than before. The way to prevent this is by keeping your wiper blades clean. They are made of exactly the same rubber material that is found in the seals around your windows. As such, they should be regularly cleaned with silicone spray to prevent them from cracking. Once again, make sure you follow the directions to the letter. By keeping your wipers in good shape, you will also make cleaning your window that much easier.

Door Locks

Most people never think of cleaning their door locks until it is too late. If you allow too much dirt and dust to accumulate inside a door lock, then eventually the tumblers inside the lock could seize. The tumblers are the small ratchet mechanisms within a lock that enable it to be opened with a key. The result is that you will be locked out of your car. Every now and then you should spray some compressed air into the lock to blow out any large particles of dirt. Compressed air is available in cans, and it is a convenient item to have around the house in order for you to clean cameras and electronic equipment, such as video cassette recorders and radios. Always read the directions on the can carefully, because using compressed air incorrectly could result in a syrupy liquid (the compressing agent) coming out of the spout. If you discover that your lock is already becoming somewhat stiff, then your tumblers are starting to seize. You should cover your key with lubricating oil (the kind used to stop hinges from squeaking, *not* motor oil), and then insert it into the lock several times. This should loosen up the tumblers sufficiently. You will probably then have to run some water over your key to remove any residual oil.

The Paint

Short of replacing your car's engine, getting your car repainted is one of the most expensive alterations you can make to an automobile. We've all seen how terrible some of those bargain paint jobs look, and even the most expensive paint job rarely rivals the one the car originally came with, so you should do your best to keep the car's paint looking like new. The simplest way to do this is to prevent it from getting damaged or dulled by the sun. Park it inside your garage whenever possible. If you must leave it outside, then consider investing in a car cover. Whenever you go out to the mall, try to park in an area with fewer car, so as to lessen the possibility of scratches and "door dings."

Lights

You should pay special attention to your car's external lights (i.e., headlights, brake lights, reverse lights) whenever you clean your car. Aside from your horn, your lights are the only method of communication that you have with other drivers, so they should be kept free from dirt and debris that could prevent other motorists from seeing them. Generally, a hose will get them as clean as can be, but if you live in a climate where there is a great deal of rain and mud, then you will probably have to wash them with soap and warm water. While you are cleaning them, you should also take the time to verify that they are still working. Have someone else press on the brake pedal, for example, while you look at the brake lights. If one or both of them fail to come on, then you should have the bulbs replaced immediately.

Convertible Roofs

Nothing beats the joy of tooling around town in a convertible. But few things are as hard to keep clean as a convertible top that is more than a few years old. Many people simply throw in the towel when faced with this challenge, opting to pay several hundred dollars or more to have the top replaced. But this is an awful lot of money to spend, especially considering how much convertibles cost in the first place. The best way to clean a convertible's top is to hose it down thoroughly. Once the water has dried, you should apply a

211

generous coating of leather or vinyl cleanser. This will return the top's shine as much as possible.

Many American cars (and a few imported cars) have simulated convertible roofs. These are especially convenient if you love the way that convertibles look, but you live in a climate too cold to allow you to purchase one. These simulated tops become discolored even more quickly than real convertible tops, so you should start taking care of them as soon as possible. Once again, hosing them down and then applying leather or vinyl cleanser is generally the best treatment. If your simulated top is already very old and discolored, then there is nothing that you can do to return its original luster short of replacing it. As with expensive rims, the price of fashion is a great deal of attention and upkeep.

Bumpers

There are two main types of bumpers these days: integrated bumpers and nonintegrated bumpers. The integrated ones are those which seem to protrude directly and seamlessly from the car's body, while the nonintegrated type are clearly differentiated from the rest of the body. If your car wears the former type, then they should be cared for in exactly the same way as you care for your car's paint job. The small black rubber areas can generally achieve a suitable shine by hosing them down. If they still seem quite dull, you can apply tire cleaner. The latter type requires a little more work. Usually, nonintegrated bumpers are made predominantly of metal, so they should be treated in much the same way as the metal components of your interior. That is, you should wipe them clean with a soft cloth. If that does not do the trick, then you can use soap and warm water (this metal is more resistant to wear than the metal found in the interior) to remove any dirt or grease. You should clean the black rubber areas with exactly the same method mentioned above. If you have any old and wrinkled bumper stickers that you want to remove, then you can purchase a special glue dissolver from drug stores or auto supply stores. After applying this agent, you should be able to work off the sticker with little resistance. You can then wipe off any residual glue with soap and warm water.

License Plates

When was the last time you took a look at your license plate? Chances are not since you put on your last registration sticker. Because of their locations, front and back license plates easily become coated with mud. This obscures the numbers and letters, and therefore makes them illegible. This defeats the whole purpose of a car wearing license plates! All you need to do is hose them down and they will be as good as new.

Hiring Help

People are finally starting to realize that organizing and managing a household is a difficult task. This task can take many hours out of your day, and when it is done best, people don't notice that it has been done at all. As such, at some point in your task of creating a well organized household, you may have to ask yourself if you need help.

At first you should try to recruit this help from family members and friends. Ask everyone to pitch in and do their fair share. Kids should not be excused from this duty, as they often feel a sense of pride at being invited to join in on "adult" activities. Besides, there's more than enough work to go around.

If you still feel that you need help, then you will probably have to hire someone. But this is an important decision, not to be taken lightly, for you are asking a stranger to come into your house. What measures can you take to find the most efficient, most trustworthy, and best qualified person for the job? This chapter will show you how to do so. Relax, because it is not as difficult as it sounds.

Making the Right Choice
Should I or Shouldn't I?

Hiring an outsider is one of the biggest organizational decisions you will have to make regarding your home. While this person may be a tremendous help with chores and watching your children, what if you feel like your home has been intruded? In the first place, you're the boss, so don't hire anyone with whom you are not entirely comfortable. In the second place, many families legitimately need outside help these days; it's getting harder and harder to raise a family on just one income.

Where Should I Go to Find Help?

There are certainly many fine agencies who can match you with a helper. They have candidates specially trained as cleaners, sitters, cooks, companions (for the sick and elderly), drivers, etc. If you need one person for a specific duty, then an agency may be appropriate for you. Simply look one up in the yellow pages. But if you need more generalized help, then why not try placing an ad at the local university job center? There are plenty of students who would love to supplement their income by returning to a "homey" environment.

The Right Person

Don't forget that you are the boss, and you have the right to choose the best person for the job. Ask questions—lots of questions. That's what "real" employers do when they interview people for a job, so why shouldn't you? You have the right to know whether or not your new employee smokes, has a work permit, has special skills, likes kids, etc. Be wary of people who simply need a place to live while settling into a new neighborhood.

Credentials

No matter how you decide to get help, always ask for references. You want someone trustworthy in your home, and no one can be trusted so implicitly if they can't even provide you with the names and numbers of three employers, teachers, or other upstanding members of the community. Also, try to find someone with related experience or a good track record.

217

For example, if you want someone to watch your kids, then perhaps look for a student who is majoring in education. Or if you want a driver, find someone whose DMV record is clean.

Reference Questions

So you've asked your prospective employee for references, and you are about to call those people on the phone, but you suddenly realize that you don't know what you're supposed to ask. Just ask for the truth. How do you know this person? Is this person trustworthy and reliable? What is this person's best quality? What is this person's worst quality? Were you happy with this person's work (ask this to a teacher or former employer, not a personal reference)? If the reference senses that you simply want honest answers, then chances are they will provide them.

Payment

In and Out

The two major classifications of hired help are those who live in and those who live out. Live in help is usually much cheaper, as most of the salary takes the form of room and board, but you lose considerably more of your privacy. This kind of help is often best reserved for sitters for young children or other jobs where 24-hour assistance could be needed. Hired help who lives out can be paid up to about three or four times as much as their live in counterparts, but you do not have to worry about feeding them or providing them with a room.

How Much?

It can be a difficult decision deciding how much you are willing to pay your help. No matter what duties they fulfill, however, a good rule of thumb is to consider any special circumstances. For example, do you have an unusually large family (for sitters), is your house particularly big (for cleaners), is it far away from town (for drivers), and do you need someone to put in extra-long days? If your answer to any of these questions, or to any similar questions, is yes, then you're going to have to offer more money. Your help should be paid every week.

Food Facts

While you cannot consider food a legitimate form of reimbursement, you should be willing to provide your employee with meals when they work. And these should be nice meals, just like the rest of the family eats. It is not adequate or fair for you to feed your help leftovers (especially if your employee is the cook!). Give your employee free access to the refrigerator, but make sure that he or she does not abuse this right. It is only natural that a well fed employee will work better.

Other Compensation

If your employee lives outside your home, then you should be prepared to pay for his or her bus fare. If he or she has a car, then pay for gas (this is especially true if you are hiring this person to run errands—in that case, you need to develop a system of monitoring gas consumption so that you are not cheated). If your employee lives in your house, then provide a nice room for him or her. The room should be welcoming, not foreboding. Have a nice little table and a nice little TV. Make sure the bed is comfortable. While this may not be your employee's home *per se*, it is not fair for you to make him or her live in uncomfortable conditions.

Taxes

Whenever you hire anyone, you have to take into account taxes. Are you going to pay their annual withholdings or are they going to have to take care of that themselves? You might also want to consider different insurance plans, such as Workman's Compensation. Contact your accountant or local Chamber of Commerce for information about these types of issues.

Budgeting

In the previous chapter, you learned a few tips about how to budget your income. If you wish to hire outside help, then naturally your budget is going to have to reflect this. Once again, be realistic about the amount of money you would need to spend hiring someone. Perhaps this is simply out of your budget. If you do have some money, but not a lot, then you can always "sweeten the deal" that you offer; how about one paid day off every month, for example? Also, remember that the more you can take care of yourself, the less time you will need someone working in your home; thus, if you personally are able to follow as many of the suggestions in this book as possible, then maybe you can hire someone part-time instead of full-time.

Rules and Training

Friends and Neighbors

If you have hired someone to work in your home, then you're going to have to give them some of the rights of anyone else in the household. Allow him or her to use the phone. Allow him or her to have friends over occasionally. Allow him or her to make slight changes in the schedule, if absolutely necessary. The key here is to lay down some strict ground rules. For example, no long distance calls before 5:00 p.m. Or no guests before noon.

Family Food

Don't make your employee guess what you like to eat. If this person is going to cook for you, then provide clear recipes. You should even go to the grocery store with him or her to make sure that they know how to find the best bargains and do not buy any brands that you do not like. It is within your rights to demand that your employee is a good cook, but you have to show that person what you consider good cooking. And it is always a nice gesture to budget a certain amount each week for foods that he or she likes.

Healthy?

It is not unreasonable to ask your new employee to get a check up. After all, you don't want anyone playing with your children who doesn't have a clean bill of health. But, you must understand that it is your responsibility to pay for such a check up, and there are certain personal matters that the employee has the right to keep to himself or herself.

Training

All new employees need training, no matter what the job, and hiring someone to help you out in your home can be very frustrating for *them*. Perhaps, for example, you don't keep the cleaning supplies where they naturally would. As such, you should give them a little bit of freedom to reorganize things within reason; this will make them more efficient in the long run. You are going to have to spend several days going over their duties with them. Watch them as they work and suggest changes as the need arises. Don't burden them with too many duties at once; perhaps show them four or five new things a day, and by the end of the first week they should have a solid idea of what is expected of them. Encourage them to ask questions. After about a month, your household should be in a routine, but try to be understanding if your employee doesn't know how to deal with every new situation. For example, perhaps he or she does not know that the outside faucets must be turned off when it starts getting cold at the end of autumn.

Outside Training

If training seems like a difficult task to you, then you are not alone. It is only when you are faced with the challenge of showing someone how to do something that you really start to understand just how difficult teaching is. One of the benefits of hiring through a professional service is that the employees are all trained by the agency. As such, they merely need to learn the idiosyncrasies of your particular home. The amount of time it takes them to learn the ropes should therefore be fairly swift.

Books Available from
Santa Monica Press

What's Buggin' You?
Michael Bohdan's Guide to
Home Pest Control
by Michael Bohdan
256 pages $12.95

Letter Writing Made Easy!
Volume 2
by Margaret McCarthy
224 pages $12.95

Offbeat Golf
A Swingin' Guide to a
Worldwide Obsession
by Bob Loeffelbein
192 pages $17.95

Heath Care Handbook
A Consumer's Guide to the
American Health Care
System
by Mark Cromer
256 pages $12.95

The Book of Good Habits
Simple and Creative Ways to
Enrich Your Life
by Dirk Mathison
224 pages $9.95

Offbeat Museums
The Curators and Collections
of America's Most Unusual
Museums
by Saul Rubin
240 pages $17.95

Helpful Household Hints
by June King
224 pages $12.95

How to Win Lotteries,
Sweepstakes, and
Contests
by Steve Ledoux
224 pages $12.95

Letter Writing Made Easy!
Featuring Sample Letters for
Hundreds of Common
Occasions
by Margaret McCarthy
224 pages $12.95

How to Find Your Family
Roots
The Complete Guide to
Searching for Your Ancestors
by William Latham
224 pages $12.95

ORDER FORM
1-800-784-9553

	Amount
	Amount
What's Buggin' You? ($12.95)	_____
Letter Writing Made Easy! Volume 2 ($12.95)	_____
Offbeat Golf ($17.95)	_____
Health Care Handbook ($12.95)	_____
The Book of Good Habits ($9.95)	_____
Offbeat Museums ($17.95)	_____
Helpful Household Hints ($12.95)	_____
How to Win Lotteries, Sweepstakes...($12.95)	_____
Letter Writing Made Easy! ($12.95)	_____
How to Find Your Family Roots ($12.95)	_____
Subtotal	_____
Shipping and Handling (see below)	_____
CA residents add 8.25% sales tax	_____
Total	_____

Name _____

Address _____

City _____ State _____ Zip _____

Card Number _____ Exp _____

_____Visa   _____MasterCard

Signature _____

Please make checks payable to: Shipping and Handling:
Santa Monica Press LLC   1 book $3.00
P.O. Box 1076   2–3 books $4.00
Santa Monica, CA 90406   Additional books $0.50